THE GREATNESS
Of
THE LAST ADAM –
HIS CREATION –
And
HIS CROSS

By
David Olander

The Greatness of the Last Adam – His Creation and His Cross

©2018 Tyndale Seminary Press

by David Olander, Ph.D, Th.D

Published by Tyndale Seminary Press
Hurst, TX

ISBN-10: 1790874645

ISBN-13: 978-1790874644

All rights reserved. No part of this publication may be reproduced, stored in a retrieval system, or transmitted in any form or by any means –electronic, mechanical, photocopy, recording, or any other – except for brief quotation in printed reviews, without the prior permission of the publisher.

All Scripture quotations, except those noted otherwise are from the New American Standard Bible,
©1960,1962,1963,1968,1971,1972,1973,1975, and 1977 by the Lockman Foundation.

Table of Contents

Chapter 1..............................5

Chapter 2.............................13

Chapter 3............................43

Chapter 4............................75

Appendix A........................123

Appendix B........................133

Appendix C........................145

Appendix D........................155

Appendix E........................169

Appendix F........................175

Introduction

"So also it is written, the first man, Adam,
became a living soul. The last Adam
became a life-giving spirit" (1 Cor. 15:45).

Absolutely nothing has come into existence in this present creation apart from Jesus Christ, the Eternal Son of God, "In the beginning God created the heavens and the earth" (Gen. 1:1). "All things came into being by Him, and apart from Him nothing came into being that has come into being" (John 1:3). He is even the Source Who is continually sustaining His own creation. "And He is before all things, and in Him all things hold together"[1] (Col. 1:17).

It is often overlooked that all things were created by Him and for Him. "For by Him all things were created, *both* in the heavens and on earth, visible and invisible, whether thrones or dominions or rulers or authorities-- all things have been created by Him and for Him" (Col. 1:16). All living beings or creatures were created by Him and for Him not only mankind but also the angelic world. All His creation was to declare His eternal glory. This is without compromise of a vast doxological principle which Scripture absolutely affirms. "The heavens are telling of the glory of God; and their expanse is declaring the work of His hands. Day to day pours forth speech, and night to night reveals knowledge" (Ps. 19:1-2). Just looking heavenward declares a perfectly righteous Creator, "And the heavens declare His righteousness,[2] For God Himself is judge"

---

[1] συνίστημι ... **to come to be in a condition of coherence,** *continue,* **endure, exist, hold together,** ... τὰ πάντα ἐν αὐτῷ συνέστηκεν **Col 1:17** William Arndt, Frederick W. Danker, and Walter Bauer, *A Greek-English Lexicon of the New Testament and Other Early Christian Literature* (Chicago: University of Chicago Press, 2000), 972–973.

[2] צֶדֶק ...noun masculine... rightness, righteousness ...administration of justice ... Ps. 50:6 Francis Brown, Samuel Rolles Driver, and Charles Augustus Briggs, *Enhanced Brown-Driver-Briggs Hebrew and English*

(Ps. 50:6).

His entire creation including mankind and the angelic realm were to bring glory and praise Him. This was not only for creating a blessed life with Him but to be with Him and have great eternal fellowship with a very gracious and loving Creator. Man was created in the image of God to have this very special fellowship with his Creator. Angels were not created in His image but were ministering spirits, "Are they not all ministering spirits, sent out to render service for the sake of those who will inherit salvation?" (Heb. 1:14). Angels were also to obey His word, "Bless the LORD, you His angels, Mighty in strength, who perform His word, obeying the voice of His word!" (Ps. 103:20). The entire creation was to praise and glorify a very wonderful and gracious Creator. All creatures were called upon to praise the name of the LORD.

> "Praise the LORD! Praise the LORD from the heavens; Praise Him in the heights! Praise Him, all His angels; Praise Him, all His hosts! Praise Him, sun and moon; Praise Him, all stars of light! Praise Him, highest heavens, and the waters that are above the heavens! Let them praise the name of the LORD, For He commanded and they were created. He has also established them forever and ever; He has made a decree which will not pass away. Praise the LORD from the earth, Sea monsters and all deeps; Fire and hail, snow and clouds; Stormy wind, fulfilling His word; Mountains and all hills; Fruit trees and all cedars; Beasts and all cattle; Creeping things and winged fowl; Kings of the earth and all peoples; Princes and all judges of the earth; Both young men and virgins; Old men and children. Let them praise the name of the LORD, for His name alone is exalted; His glory is above earth and heaven. And He has lifted up a horn for His people, Praise for all His godly ones; *Even* for the sons of Israel, a people near to Him. Praise the LORD!" (Ps. 148).

Lexicon (Oxford: Clarendon Press, 1977), 841. God administers justice in His creation flawlessly. On day in the kingdom His justice will seen in all the earth.

Sin actually started in heaven with the angelic host. Part of the angelic realm chose against their Creator with their leader Satan who not only wanted to rule as God but be God (Is. 14:12-16; Ezek. 28:11-19). The devil or Satan and his angels[3] sinned against God prior to the sin of Adam. However, Adam with his God-given free will chose not to obey and glorify his Creator. Satan challenged Adam that he could be like God.

> "THE DERIVATION OF SIN The terms *evil* and *sin* represent somewhat different ideas. *Evil* may refer to that which, though latent or not expressed, is ever conceivable as the opposite of that which is good, while *sin* is that which is concrete and actively opposed to the character of God. It is difficult for the human mind to depict a time when there was not an opposite to good even though, for want of beings who were capable of sinning, it could have had no opportunity of expression. But since God cannot err, sin could not come into existence until another form of being was created; and, apparently, following upon God's creative act, the highest of angels sinned, as did also the first man."[4]

Man was created in the image of God and given a holy estate to reign with and under his Creator. Adam was told that if he ate from the tree of the knowledge of good and evil he would die (Gen. 2:17). Adam was no puppet without volition or will but he was created with 'free will' that is a contrary

---

[3] The devil or Satan and his angels were allowed by God, in His great sovereignty, this rebellion against His infinitely perfect nature. The lake of fire or eternal hell was never prepared for man but for the devil and his angels. "Then He will also say to those on His left, 'Depart from Me, accursed ones, into **the eternal fire which has been prepared for the devil and his angels**" (Mat. 25:41); τότε ἐρεῖ καὶ τοῖς ἐξ εὐωνύμων· πορεύεσθε ἀπ' ἐμοῦ [οἱ] κατηραμένοι εἰς τὸ πῦρ τὸ αἰώνιον τὸ **ἡτοιμασμένον** τῷ διαβόλῳ καὶ τοῖς ἀγγέλοις αὐτοῦ. Note the perfect participle for 'prepared.' "And the great dragon was thrown down, the serpent of old who is called **the devil and Satan**, who deceives the whole world; he was thrown down to the earth, **and his angels** were thrown down with him" (Rev 12:9).

[4] Lewis Sperry Chafer, *Systematic Theology*, vol. 2 (Grand Rapids, MI: Kregel Publications, 1993), 228.

nature which was able to choose against God. This was not sin in itself, but man used his God given free will to choose against His Creator (Gen. 1-3).[5] The creature not only chose willfully and defiantly against His Creator, but he chose to listen to the godless wisdom of a fallen angel, that is Satan in lieu of his Creator. The world became subject to the wrath of God because of man's sin not angelic sin: "For as in Adam all die" (1 Cor. 15:22). Man was created in God's image, angels were not. And death came into the world through the one man Adam: "Therefore, just as through one man sin entered into the world, and death through sin, and so death spread to all men, because all sinned" (Rom. 5:12). God sees the whole world as having sinned in Adam.[6]

All men are fully aware of God's creation and are fully accountable to God for understanding there is a Creator. But, they suppress His truth willfully even though He is reaching out in love and grace to all men. "For the wrath of God is revealed from heaven against all ungodliness and unrighteousness of men, who suppress the truth in unrighteousness, because that which is known about God is evident within them; for God made it evident to them. For since the creation of the world His invisible attributes, His eternal power and divine nature, have been clearly seen, being understood through what has been made, so that they are without excuse" (Rom 1:18).

Yet God still showed His love and grace by sending His own eternal Son to die for all men's sin. "For God so loved the

---

[5] Man was created with a nature that was able to choose against his Creator i.e. man was created with contrary choice which is not sin in itself. Man sinned by not only choosing against God but his declaration of independence from his Creator, he no longer wanted God in his life.

[6] "And, so to speak, through Abraham even Levi, who received tithes, paid tithes" (Heb. 7:9). This is comparable to Adam's sin and how 'all sinned in Adam' (Rom. 5:12). It is important to note how God sees this, not man. He sees Levi as paying tithes through Abraham though Levi did as not yet exist. God sees the whole race sinning in Adam as a race not individually as pre-existing but as the whole human race. This issue will be more thoroughly addressed in chapter 5.

world, that He gave His only begotten Son, that whoever believes in Him should not perish, but have eternal life" (John 3:16). God loves the world of very sinful men, *all* sinful men. "But God demonstrates His own love toward us, in that while we were yet sinners, Christ died for us" (Rom. 5:8). He took on a human nature yet without sin to die for the sin of the world (John 1:29; Phil. 2:5-11). "It is thus demonstrated that the *incarnation* is of surpassing importance. Whatever momentousness belongs to the doctrine of Christ's *Deity* or to the doctrine of His *humanity*, the doctrine of the *incarnation* includes both; even later studies of the hypostatic union and the kenosis will serve only to elucidate the fuller meaning of the *incarnation*."[7]

The greatness of the last Adam, His creation, and His work on the cross is nothing less than pure grace. God displayed His love mercy and grace by the permission of sin into His perfect creation.

> "Many are the attempts made by those who understand nothing of the real character of God to save Him from the undesirable reputation He must acquire if He does not in compassion rescue all beings from eternal retribution. Such is the doctrinal confusion which arises when one truth is stressed without regard for other truths which qualify it. God is holiness and righteousness as well as love. It is the holiness of His Person and the righteousness of His government which preclude Him from any mere generosity which would make light of sin. In fact, sin is sufficiently sinful to require eternal retribution as the divine penalty for it. There is no field for argument at this point. The Word of God must stand and man must be reminded that of the two issues involved—sin and holiness—he knows nothing about their depth of meaning. Being *absolute*, divine holiness cannot be varied or altered in the least degree. This truth is the key to the entire problem which the idea of retribution engenders. If God could have forgiven one sin of one person as an act of mere kindness, He would have compromised His own holiness which demands judgment for sin. Having thus compromised Himself with sin, He would need Himself to be saved because of the unrighteous thing He had done. He would,

---

[7] Lewis Sperry Chafer, *Systematic Theology*, vol. 1 (Grand Rapids, MI: Kregel Publications, 1993), 364.

by such supposed kindness, have established a principle by which He could forgive all human sin as an act of divine clemency, and thus the death of Christ is rendered unnecessary. This truth must not be overlooked if the doctrine of eternal retribution is to be understood at all. Let it be restated that, if God could save one soul from one sin by mere generosity, He could save all souls from sin by generosity and the death of Christ thus becomes the greatest possible divine blunder. It is the fact of unyielding divine holiness which demands either the retribution of the sinner or the death of Christ in his room and stead. God is love, and that love is demonstrated by the gift of the Son that men might be saved; but love and mercy did not circumvent the demands of holiness to save the sinner: they paid its every demand. The conclusion of the matter is that God, because of His holiness, cannot save the lost unless His holy demands are met for the sinner, as they are met in the death of Christ; and to be unsaved, or outside the grace of God as it is in Christ, is to be destined to eternal retribution. God can do no more than to provide a perfect salvation, which is provided at infinite cost. When love will pay such a price that a sinner may be saved and holiness remain untarnished, it ill becomes finite men to tamper with these immutable realities. Those who resent the idea of eternal retribution are, in fact, resenting divine holiness. However, the message of God's grace to sinful men is not merely a proclamation of eternal condemnation; it is rather that the chief of sinners may be saved through the Savior that infinite love has provided.[8]

    This book is about the greatness of the last Adam not only as the Creator but the One who completely obeyed the Father's will and died for the sin of the world. Although He is the eternal Son of God, He emptied Himself taking the form of a servant to die for all men's sin. Chapter 2 is a study of Jesus Who is the eternal Son. "Now after Jesus was born in Bethlehem of Judea in the days of Herod the king, behold, magi from the east arrived in Jerusalem, saying, Where is He who has been born King of the Jews? For we saw His star in the east, and have come to worship Him" (Mat. 2:1-2). Jesus never worshiped God for He is eternally God, the eternal Son of God. Jesus is to be worshiped for He is God, the Son of God.
    Chapter 3 presents God the Son and His creation. It is

---

[8] Ibid. 432–433.

should continually be kept in focus that He is the last Adam and created the first Adam. He is the Creator of everything both man and angels, and it is important to deal with fallen angels. There is much misinformation about them especially 'angelic cohabitation.' Chapter 4 presents a study concerning this issue. And chapter 5 compares the work of the first Adam to the greatness of the last Adam.

There are 7 appendices at the end of the book, and it would be good for the reader to work through each one individually. They are individually referenced in the book, but it would behoove the reader to study each one for a good understanding of each issue being presented. All these appendices are critical for a good comprehension of the Text.

Appendix A concerns the expression 'in the beginning.' "In the beginning God created the heavens and the earth' and surprisingly there is a great deal of debate about this and the Hebrew construction. Appendix B addresses 'formless and void' and Appendix C deals directly with Isaiah 45:18. Appendix D shows that the words <u>create</u> בָּרָא and <u>made</u> עָשָׂה are used synonymously. Appendix E clarifies the importance of Hebrews 1:2 and 11:3. Finally Appendix F explains the expression 'the sons of God' primarily from the book of Job.

The authority, infallibility, and inerrancy of Scripture have to be the priority for all information concerning these issues. Without God's inerrant word man would know nothing of the greatness of the last Adam.

> "The Bible's authority is demonstrated, also, in that it is accurate to the degree of infinity in matters of history and prophecy. Historical data set forth in the original writings are inerrant, and prophecy not only discloses the oncoming events of the future, but provides unfailing assurance that all that is predicted will be executed by the sovereign and therefore irresistible competency of God. Thus has the divine authority of the Scriptures been demonstrated in the grand array of predictions already fulfilled, and thus it will be demonstrated in the plenary realization of all that is yet unfulfilled. "The zeal of the LORD of hosts will perform this."[9]

---

[9] Ibid. 103.

"Since there can be no saving relation to God apart from the redemption which Christ has accomplished, His death becomes the ground of nearly all aspects of Christian truth."[10] There is nothing grander in this life than to believe and study the Person and the greatness of the last Adam.

---

[10] Lewis Sperry Chafer, *Systematic Theology*, vol. 5 (Grand Rapids, MI: Kregel Publications, 1993), 177.

The Eternal Son of God

Jesus Christ, the Eternal Son of God

The greatest question ever asked of any man in this age is 'who is Jesus Christ?' The greatest question ever asked of Jesus Christ is 'are you the Son of God'?

- "But Jesus kept silent. And the high priest said to Him, I adjure You by the living God, that You tell us whether You are the Christ, **the Son of God**. Jesus said to him, you have said it *yourself*; nevertheless I tell you, hereafter you shall see the Son of Man sitting at the right hand of Power, and coming on the clouds of heaven. Then the high priest tore his robes, saying, He has blasphemed! What further need do we have of witnesses? Behold, you have now heard the blasphemy" (Mat. 26:63-65).

- "Are You **the Son of God** and He said to them, Yes, I am" (Luke 22:70).

- "The Jews answered him, we have a law, and by that law He ought to die because He made Himself out *to be* **the Son of God**" (John 19:7)

The gospels clearly teach He is the eternal Son of God

"He trusts in God; let Him deliver *Him* now, if He takes pleasure in Him; for He said, I am the Son of God"[1] (Mat.

---

[1] Note the Greek statement that this is an "I am" proclamation: πέποιθεν ἐπὶ τὸν θεόν, ῥυσάσθω νῦν εἰ θέλει αὐτόν· εἶπεν γὰρ ὅτι **θεοῦ εἰμι υἱός**. He is

27:43). Mark begins His gospel with the message concerning Jesus Christ, the Son of God. "The beginning of the gospel of Jesus Christ, the Son of God" (Mark 1:1). "And the angel answered and said to her, "The Holy Spirit will come upon you, and the power of the Most High will overshadow you; and for that reason the holy offspring shall be called the Son of God" (Luke 1:35).[2] John makes it exceptionally clear that he wrote his gospel for one very important reason. "Many other signs therefore Jesus also performed in the presence of the disciples, which are not written in this book; but these have been written that you may believe that Jesus is the Christ, the Son of God; and that believing you may have life in His name" (John 20:30-31).[3] His name is referring to His very person that He is the Son of God. The Son is the true God and eternal life (1 John 5:20).[4] Jesus never became the Son of God for He is the true God, eternal Jehovah in the flesh.

---

continually and eternally the Son. He did not become the Son of God in any sense. This is one of the greatest 'I am' statements and He is on the cross for this, and it is being thrown back at Him at the crucifixion.

[2] "**Mary** did not seem surprised that the Messiah was to come. Rather, she was surprised that she would be His mother since she was **a virgin** (lit., "since I do not know a man"). But **the angel** did not rebuke Mary, as he had rebuked Zechariah (v. 20). This indicates that Mary did not doubt the angel's words but merely wanted to know how such an event would be accomplished. The answer was that **the Holy Spirit** would creatively bring about the physical conception of Jesus (v. 35). This miraculous conception and Virgin Birth of Jesus Christ was necessary because of His deity and preexistence (cf. Isa. 7:14; 9:6; Gal. 4:4)." John A. Martin, "Luke," in *The Bible Knowledge Commentary: An Exposition of the Scriptures*, ed. J. F. Walvoord and R. B. Zuck, vol. 2 (Wheaton, IL: Victor Books, 1985), 205.

[3] Only by believing Who He truly is and what He did would anyone have life in His name. He is the Son of God, literally Jehovah in the flesh and He died for our sins and was raised on the 3rd day (1 Cor. 15:1-4).

[4] "And we know that **the Son of God** has come, and has given us understanding, in order that we might know Him who is true, and we are in Him who is true, in **His Son Jesus Christ**. **This is the true God and eternal life**" (1 John 5:20)

Jesus was worshipped as a child

Only God is to be worshipped and it is important to note that as a child the magi worshipped Him. "Where is He who has been born King of the Jews? For we saw His star in the east, and have come to worship Him" (Mat. 2:2). Only God is to be worshipped.[5] "Therefore the Lord Himself will give you a sign: Behold, a virgin will be with child and bear a son, and she will call His name Immanuel" (Isaiah 7:14); "Behold, the virgin shall be with child, and shall bear a Son, and they shall call His name Immanuel, which translated means, God with us" (Mat. 1:3). This is literally Jehovah with us and this is literally Jehovah incarnate or in the flesh. Only Jehovah is to be worshipped.

This was the Son of God in the flesh as a babe and was to be worshipped for this babe is Jehovah God, the God-man, the eternal Son of God. "And the angel answered and said to her, The Holy Spirit will come upon you, and the power of the Most High will overshadow you; and for that reason the holy offspring shall be called **the Son of God**" (Luke 1:35). "In the case of the Lord Jesus Christ, the Incarnate Word, the process is the miraculous conception of Immanuel in the womb of the Virgin Mary. God delicately shrouds the mechanics of the process in mystery, revealing only that "The Holy Spirit shall come upon thee, and the power of the Most High shall overshadow thee ..." (Luke 1:35) and "... that which is conceived in her is of the Holy Spirit" (Matt. 1:20). In this process God was united with a human being who was a sinner

---

[5] "You shall fear *only* the LORD your God; and you shall worship Him, and swear by His name" (Dt. 6:13); "And it shall come about if you ever forget the LORD your God, and go after other gods and serve them and worship them, I testify against you today that you shall surely perish. (Dt. 8:19); "Then Jesus said to him, Begone, Satan! For it is written, You shall worship the Lord your God, and serve Him only" (Mat 4:10). "And he said with a loud voice, Fear God, and give Him glory, because the hour of His judgment has come; and worship Him who made the heaven and the earth and sea and springs of waters" (Rev. 14:7). Jesus is the Creator and is to be worshipped for He is the Son of God.

by nature and by practice (we admit the immaculate conception of the Lord Jesus Christ, but we deny the Roman Catholic dogma of the immaculate conception of Mary), but who was a willing instrument in the hand of God (cf. Luke 1:38). The product of this process is the Incarnate Word, the theanthropic Person, the one described as "the holy thing" (Luke 1:35), without sin (John 8:46; Heb. 4:15). In the case of the Scriptures, the written Word, the process is the miraculous conception of the very words of God in the minds of the human authors. God likewise shrouds the mechanics of this process in mystery, revealing only that the human authors were "… being moved by the Holy Spirit" (2 Pet. 1:21). In this process God was united with human beings who were sinners by nature and by practice, but who were willing instruments in the hands of God (2 Pet. 1:21). The product of this process is the written Word, the theanthropic Book, the volume described as "the holy scriptures" (2 Tim. 3:15, A. V.), without error."[6]

John the baptizer proclaimed He was the Son of God

"The next day he saw Jesus coming to him, and said, "Behold, the Lamb of God who takes away the sin of the world! This is He on behalf of whom I said, after me comes a Man who has a higher rank than I, for He existed before me. And I did not recognize Him, but in order that He might be manifested to Israel, I came baptizing in water. And John bore witness saying, I have beheld the Spirit descending as a dove out of heaven, and He remained upon Him. And I did not recognize Him, but He who sent me to baptize in water said to me, 'He upon whom you see the Spirit descending and remaining upon Him, this is the one who baptizes in the Holy

---

[6] John A. Witmer, "The Incarnate and the Written Word of God," *Bibliotheca Sacra* 113 (1956): 68–69.

Spirit. And I have seen, and have <u>borne witness that **this** is the Son of God.</u>"[7]
(John 1:29-34).

The apostles knew He was God's Son, the eternal Son of God

"Nathanael answered Him, Rabbi, You are the Son of God; You are the King of Israel" (John 1:49). "And immediately He made the disciples get into the boat, and go ahead of Him to the other side, while He sent the multitudes away. And after He had sent the multitudes away, He went up to the mountain by Himself to pray; and when it was evening, He was there alone. But the boat was already many stadia away from the land, battered by the waves; for the wind was contrary. And in the fourth watch of the night He came to them, walking on the sea. And when the disciples saw Him walking on the sea, they were frightened, saying, It is a ghost! And they cried <u>out for fear. But immediately</u> Jesus spoke to them, saying, Take

---

[7] "And I have seen, and have borne witness that **this is the Son of God**" (John 1:34). Note the construction of John's testimony or witness which is in the perfect indicative that Jesus is continually the Son of God: κἀγὼ ἑώρακα καὶ μεμαρτύρηκα ὅτι **οὗτός ἐστιν ὁ υἱὸς τοῦ θεοῦ.** "**I have seen** (ἑωρακα [*heōraka*]). Present perfect active of ὁραω [*horaō*]. John repeats the statement of verse 32 (τεθεαμαι [*tetheamai*]). **Have borne witness** (μεμαρτυρηκα [*memartureka*]). Perfect active indicative of μαρτυρεω [*martureō*] for which verb see 32. **This is the Son of God** (ὁ υἱος του θεου [*ho huios tou theou*]). The Baptist saw the Spirit come on Jesus at his baptism and undoubtedly heard the Father's voice hail him as "My Beloved Son" (Mark 1:11=Matt. 3:17=Luke 3:22). Nathanael uses it as a Messianic title (John 1:49) as does Martha (11:27). The Synoptics use it also of Christ (Mark 3:11; Matt. 14:33; Luke 22:70). Caiaphas employs it to Christ as a Messianic title (Matt. 26:63) and Jesus confessed under oath that he was (verse 64), thus applying the term to himself as he does in John's Gospel (5:25; 10:36; 11:4) and by implication (the Father, the Son) in Matt. 11:27 (=Luke 10:22). Hence in the Synoptics also Jesus calls himself the Son of God. The phrase means more than just Messiah and expresses the peculiar relation of the Son to the Father (John 3:18; 5:25; 17:5; 19:7; 20:31) like that of the Logos with God in 1:1." A.T. Robertson, <u>Word Pictures in the New Testament</u> (Nashville, TN: Broadman Press, 1933), Jn 1:34–35.

courage, it is I; do not be afraid. And Peter answered Him and said, Lord, if it is You, command me to come to You on the water. And He said, Come! And Peter got out of the boat, and walked on the water and came toward Jesus. But seeing the wind, he became afraid, and beginning to sink, he cried out, saying, Lord, save me! And immediately Jesus stretched out His hand and took hold of him, and said to him, O you of little faith, why did you doubt? And when they got into the boat, the wind stopped. And those who were in the boat worshiped[8] Him, saying, **You are certainly God's Son!**" (Mat. 14:22-33). "And the Lord *said* to him, Arise and go to the street called Straight, and inquire at the house of Judas for a man from Tarsus named Saul, for behold, he is praying… Now for several days he was with the disciples who were at Damascus, and immediately he *began* to proclaim Jesus in the synagogues, saying, **He is the Son of God**" (Acts 9:11-20).

He proved to be the Son of God by the inerrant Word

Jesus proved Himself many times to be the Son of God. This was not only confirmed by signs, miracles, and wonders (Acts 2:22-23), but also by God's Word. By not believing the Son of God, many were rejecting not only Him but the inerrant Word of God. This seems to be true today in many cases.

> "The Jews took up stones again to stone Him. Jesus answered them, I showed you many good works from the Father; for which of them

---

[8] Only God is to be worshipped: "Ascribe to the LORD the glory due His name; Bring an offering, and come before Him; Worship the LORD in holy array" (1 Chr. 16:29); "You shall fear *only* the LORD your God; and you shall worship Him, and swear by His name" (Dt. 6:13); "Then Jesus said to him, Begone, Satan! For it is written, you shall worship the Lord your God, and serve Him only" (Mat. 4:10); "And Jesus answered and said to him, It is written, you shall worship the Lord your God and serve Him only" (Luke 4:8).

are you stoning Me? The Jews answered Him, for a good work we do not stone You, but for blasphemy; and because You, being a man, make Yourself out *to be* God. Jesus answered them, has it not been written in your Law, I said, you are gods? **If he called them gods, to whom the word of God came (<u>and the Scripture cannot be broken</u>), do you say of Him, whom the Father sanctified and sent into the world, You are blaspheming, because I said, <u>I am the Son of God?</u> If I do not do the works of My Father, do not believe Me; but if I do them, though you do not believe Me, believe the works, that you may know and understand that the Father is in Me, and I in the Father"** (John 10:31-38).

Only those living at the time of Christ saw His miracles. They knew He could do signs, miracles, and wonders for this confirmed Him and His message (Acts 2:22-23).[9] But there is something even greater which confirmed Him then and even today, and that is the inerrant Word of God which cannot be 'broken.'[10] "The other passage is John 10:33–36 where the Lord

---

[9] "Men of Israel, listen to these words: Jesus the Nazarene, a man attested to you by God with miracles and wonders and signs which God performed through Him in your midst, just as you yourselves know-- this *Man*, delivered up by the predetermined plan and foreknowledge of God, you nailed to a cross by the hands of godless men and put *Him* to death" (Act 2:22).

[10] The Scriptures are indestructible and teach only truth. "If he called them gods, to whom the word of God came (and the Scripture cannot be **broken**)" (John 10:35) εἰ ἐκείνους εἶπεν θεοὺς πρὸς οὓς ὁ λόγος τοῦ θεοῦ ἐγένετο, καὶ οὐ δύναται **λυθῆναι** ἡ γραφή, (Joh 10:35 BNT) **Λύω**... **to do away with, destroy, bring to an end, abolish** ...**J 5:18** (in John, Jesus is accused not of breaking the Sabbath, but of doing away w. it as an ordinance). ... **10:35** ...[**J 10:34–6**]).—λύειν τὸν Ἰησοῦν annul (the true teaching about) *Jesus* (by spurning it). William Arndt, Frederick W. Danker, and Walter Bauer, *A Greek-English Lexicon of the New Testament and Other Early Christian*

states that the Scripture cannot be broken. This is an assertion that the entire Scripture cannot be broken and that the particular words being quoted on that occasion cannot be broken. This is only possible because the Scripture is true in each particular and in all its parts."[11]

Christ Himself spoke of the inerrancy of the Text. Christ pointed not only to His works 'if I do not do the works of My Father, do not believe Me; but if I do them, though you do not believe Me, believe the works, that you may know and understand that the Father is in Me, and I in the Father' but the greater witness of His Person. "Another affirmation of great significance is John 10:33–36, where Christ states, "The scripture cannot be broken." Note first of all that Christ introduces this statement in connection with a relatively insignificant quotation from Psalm 82:6. The Lord is saying, because this portion of the Psalm is a part of Scripture and Scripture cannot be broken, neither can this portion be broken. Furthermore, He builds His whole argument on the consequent reliability of the Old Testament quotation. Secondly, notice that it is the words which are written in the Old Testament that are designated as Scripture; and because they are Scripture, they must be accepted; for they cannot be broken or nullified. The fact is, the truth expressed by the Scripture is such that, despite what men do, it will always have binding force. Thirdly, note carefully that He does not say "this Scripture" but simply "Scripture." The point is that Scripture as a whole stands inviolate and infallible."[12]

To reject Jesus Christ as the eternal Son of God is tantamount to rejecting His inerrant Word. God's Word is sure, and the Scripture cannot be broken.

Literature (Chicago: University of Chicago Press, 2000), 607.
[11] Charles C. Ryrie, "The Importance of Inerrancy," *Bibliotheca Sacra* 120 (1963): 143.
[12] W. Robert Cook, "Biblical Inerrancy and Intellectual Honesty," *Bibliotheca Sacra* 125 (1968): 169.

Demons knew He was the Son of God

The entire demonic world knows exactly who He is. "And the tempter came and said to Him, If You are **the Son of God**,[13] command that these stones become bread. But He answered and said, it is written, man shall not live on bread alone, but on every word that proceeds out of the mouth of God. Then the devil took Him into the holy city; and he had Him stand on the pinnacle of the temple, and said to Him, If You are **the Son of God** throw Yourself down; for it is written He will give His angels charge concerning You; and On *their* hands they will bear You up, Lest You strike Your foot against a stone" (Mat. 4:3-6). "And whenever the unclean spirits beheld Him, they would fall down before Him and cry out, saying, You are **the Son of God**!" (Mark 3:11). The entire satanic world is well aware of Jesus being the eternal Son of God.

The charge of blasphemy

Jesus the Son of God LORD Jehovah יְהוָה

The actual charge of blasphemy against Jesus Christ was that He claimed to be the Son of God. "The Jews answered him, we have a law, and by that law He ought to die because He made Himself out *to be* the Son of God" (John 19:7). This was the actual charge against Jesus Christ for His death. Pilate was going to let Him go because he found no fault in Him (John

---

[13] It must be noted that all these 'if' clauses are first class conditional clauses and assumed as true. This also confirms the demons knew exactly the true nature and person of the Christ.

19:6).[14] He was crucified on the political charge[15] not the actual charge of blasphemy (19:12-19). "There they crucified Him, and with Him two other men, one on either side, and Jesus in between. And Pilate wrote an inscription also, and put it on the cross. And it was written, JESUS THE NAZARENE, THE KING OF THE JEWS" (John 19:18-19). This was the political charge which might also be called sedition.

Many do not realize the actual charges against the eternal and true Son of God. "The Jewish leaders displayed their hatred of Jesus and **shouted** for His death. Crucifixion was a shameful death, usually reserved for criminals, slaves, and

---

[14] **Pilate brings Jesus before the populace.** The scourging was a pitiless Roman atrocity, often itself fatal, 1. Pilate's words, 'Behold here is the man!' 5, recalls Zechariah's prophecy: 'Here is the man whose name is the Branch' (Zech 6:12), and John the Baptist's words: 'Look, the Lamb of God, who takes away the sin of the world!' (Jn 1:29). What shame and mockery were heaped upon Him who was the God-Man, especially the crown of thorns, the emblem of the curse being borne by Him who would someday come into His kingdom by bearing the curse of sin (Rev 19:12). Verse 7 reveals the full blind unbelief of the Jews: 'He claimed to be the Son of God' (cf. Lev 24:16). Verse 15, 'We have no king but Caesar,' uncovers the full terrible apostasy of the nation. The 'Pavement' (Aramaic *Gabbatha)*, 13, was an exquisite inlaid floor, 2,500 meters square, designed as a parade ground for Roman military pomp and as the approach to the procurator's judgment hall. It was near the ancient Tower of Antonia, apparently part of the NW part of the temple area, now located under the present-day Church of the Dames de Sion. Merrill Frederick Unger, *The New Unger's Bible Handbook*, Rev. and updated ed. (Chicago: Moody Publishers, 2005), 462.

[15] Pilate found nothing wrong with Jesus as a criminal or for anything and tried to release Him. "As a result of this Pilate made efforts to release Him, but the Jews cried out, saying, If you release this Man, you are no friend of Caesar; everyone who makes himself out *to be* a king opposes Caesar" (John 19:12); "They therefore cried out, Away with *Him*, away with *Him*, crucify Him! Pilate said to them, Shall I crucify your King? The chief priests answered, We have no king but Caesar" (John 19:15); "There they crucified Him, and with Him two other men, one on either side, and Jesus in between. And Pilate wrote an inscription also, and put it on the cross. And it was written, JESUS THE NAZARENE, THE KING OF THE JEWS" (John 19:18-19). He was crucified for offering the covenanted kingdom to Israel, and He as their King.

especially revolutionaries. **Pilate** at first refused to be the executioner, but then the leaders brought forth their real reason: **He claimed to be the Son of God. According to** the **Law** the charge of blasphemy (Lev. 24:16)[16] called for death, if it could be proven."[17]

The phrase Son of God is the declaration and affirmation of His divine eternal Sonship. By saying Jesus is the Son of God meant nothing less than He is the eternal Jehovah of *all* Scripture and *all* creation.[18] This is identical to saying that Jesus is LORD the eternal Son of God. One does not "make" Jesus LORD of one's life for salvation which is a very grave misunderstanding of the Text. When one confesses Jesus is LORD biblically, he/she is saying Jesus is the Son of God which means He is Jehovah. This is exactly what His opponents knew He was saying. This is exactly the meaning of Rom. 10:9-10. "That if you confess with your mouth Jesus *as* LORD, and believe in your heart that God raised Him from the dead, you shall be saved; for with the heart man believes, resulting in righteousness, and with the mouth he confesses, resulting in salvation" (Rom. 10:9-10).[19] Note the context of

---

[16] "Moreover, the one who blasphemes the name of the LORD shall surely be put to death; all the congregation shall certainly stone him. The alien as well as the native, when he blasphemes the Name, shall be put to death" (Lev. 24:16).

[17] Edwin A. Blum, "John," in *The Bible Knowledge Commentary: An Exposition of the Scriptures*, ed. J. F. Walvoord and R. B. Zuck, vol. 2 (Wheaton, IL: Victor Books, 1985), 338.

[18] "All things came into being by Him, and apart from Him nothing came into being that has come into being" (John 1:3). πάντα δι' αὐτοῦ ἐγένετο, καὶ χωρὶς αὐτοῦ ἐγένετο οὐδὲ ἕν. ὃ γέγονεν. Nothing has come into existence apart from the Son of God for He is LORD of creation.

[19] "The evidence of Scripture is so complete that one who denies the deity of Christ must necessarily reject the accuracy of the Scriptures. Berkhof summarizes the evidence for the deity of Christ in these words: "We find that Scripture (1) *explicitly asserts the deity of the Son* in such passages as John 1:1; 20:28; Rom. 9:5; Phil. 2:6; Tit. 2:13; 1 John 5:20; (2) *applies divine names to Him*, Isa. 9:6; 40:3; Jer. 23:5, 6; **Joel 2:32** (comp. Acts 2:21); 1 Tim. 3:16; (3) *ascribes to Him divine attributes*, such as eternal existence, Isa. 9:6; John 1:1, 2; Rev. 1:8; 22:13, omnipresence, Matt. 18:20;

Rom. 10:9-10 (in the paragraph of 10:5-13). The same way one would call on the LORD for deliverance from danger or judgment especially during the day of the Lord (Joel 2:32),[20] he/she is instructed to call or invoke the person of Jesus as LORD for salvation i.e. eternal life.

"All who call on the name of the LORD יְהוָה will be delivered (Joel 2:32)."[21] Confess in Romans 10:9 is to literally say the same thing God's inerrant Word declares concerning the Son of God. The context of 10:9 is in the paragraph of 10:5-13. The context gives the true essence of what Jesus is Lord means.

- "That if you confess with your mouth **Jesus *as* Lord**, and believe in your heart that God raised Him from the dead, you shall be saved" (Rom. 10:9)[22]

28:20; John 3:13, omniscience, John 2:24, 25; 21:17; Rev. 2:23, omnipotence, Isa. 9:6; Phil. 3:21; Rev. 1:8, immutability, Heb. 1:10–12; 13:8, and in general every attribute belonging to the Father, Col. 2:9; (4) *speaks of Him as doing divine works*, as creation, John 1:3, 10; Col. 1:16; Heb. 1:2, 10, providence, Luke 10:22; John 3:35; 17:2; Eph. 1:22; Col. 1:17; Heb. 1:3, the forgiveness of sins, Matt. 9:2–7; Mark 2:7–10; Col. 3:13, resurrection and judgment, Matt. 25:31, 32; John 5:19–29; Acts 10:42; 17:31; Phil. 3:21; 2 Tim. 4:1, the final dissolution and renewal of all things, Heb. 1:10–12; Phil. 3:21; Rev. 21:5, and (5) *accords Him divine honour*, John 5:22, 23; 14:1; 1 Cor. 15:19; 2 Cor. 13:13; Heb. 1:6; Matt. 28:19." L. Berkhof, *Systematic Theology*, pp. 94–95; John F. Walvoord, "The Person of the Incarnate Christ," *Bibliotheca Sacra* 117 (1960): 101.

[20] See this author's book on '

[21] "And it will come about that whoever calls on the name of the LORD בְּשֵׁם יְהוָה will be delivered; For on Mount Zion and in Jerusalem There will be those who escape, As the LORD has said, Even among the survivors whom the LORD calls" (Joel 2:32)

[22] "That if you **confess** with your mouth Jesus *as* Lord, and believe in your heart that God raised Him from the dead, you shall be saved" (Romans 10:9). ὅτι ἐὰν **ὁμολογήσῃς** ἐν τῷ στόματί σου κύριον Ἰησοῦν καὶ πιστεύσῃς ἐν τῇ καρδίᾳ σου ὅτι ὁ θεὸς αὐτὸν ἤγειρεν ἐκ νεκρῶν, σωθήσῃ· Salvation is based on believing Who He is. Jesus is LORD, the eternal Son of God, and He died for man's sin and was raised on the 3rd day. Salvation is all about Him, not what man does. He did it all, He paid it all, all to Him we owe.

- "For **whoever will call upon the name of the LORD will be saved**" (Rom. 10:13; ref Joel 2:32)
- "And it will come about that **whoever calls on the name of the LORD Will be delivered**; For on Mount Zion and in Jerusalem There will be those who escape, As the LORD has said, Even among the survivors whom the LORD calls" (Joel 2:32)
- That if you confess with your mouth **Jesus *as* Lord (Rom. 10:9)**
- **whoever calls on the name of the LORD (Joel 2:32)**

- Call or confess the LORD Jesus for salvation (Rom. 10:9)
- Call on the LORD Jehovah יְהוָה for deliverance (Joel 2:32; Rom. 10:13)
- Calling on the LORD Jesus is saying Jesus is LORD יְהוָה
- One must believe Jesus is LORD יְהוָה for salvation, eternal life

"That if you **confess with your mouth Jesus *as* Lord**, and believe in	For **whoever will call upon the name of the LORD will be saved**" (Rom.

Man does nothing but believe for salvation i.e. Who He is and what He did (1 Cor. 15:1-4).

your heart that God raised Him from the dead, you shall be saved" (Rom. 10:9)	10:13; ref Joel 2:32)
"And it will come about that **whoever calls on the name of the LORD Will be delivered**; For on Mount Zion and in Jerusalem There will be those who escape, As the LORD has said, Even among the survivors whom the LORD calls" (Joel 2:32)	

confess with your mouth Jesus *as* **Lord**, (Rom. 10:9)	whoever will call upon the name of the **LORD** (Rom. 10:13)
whoever calls on the name of the **LORD** **JEHOVAH** יְהוָה (Joel 2:32)	

Note: that confessing **Jesus *as* Lord (Jehovah, יְהוָה) (Rom. 10:9) is the same as calling on the name of the LORD (Joel 2:32).** Context fully supports this.

"Crucial to a correct interpretation of Romans 10:9 is an understanding of the meaning of the Greek word κύριος ("Lord"). In the New Testament the word κύριος has several meanings. It is used (a) of an owner (Luke 19:33); (b) of a master, that is, one to whom service is due (Matt. 6:24); (c) of an emperor or king (Acts 25:26); (d) of idols, ironically (1 Cor. 8:5); (e) as a title of respect (Matt. 21:30) or courtesy (John 12:21); and (f) as the equivalent of the Hebrew Yahweh, the august name of God. Matthew 4:7 is an example of the sixth meaning: "Do not put the Lord your God to the test." This is a quotation from Deuteronomy 6:16, which has the word Yahweh. So Jesus was referring to Himself as God. Examples of direct quotations from the Old Testament that translate the Hebrew יהוה ("Yahweh") by the Greek word κύριος and thereby declare Jesus is Yahweh can be found throughout the New Testament (e.g., cf. Isa. 40:3 with Matt. 3:3; Ps. 110:1 with Acts 2:34–35; Joel 2:32 with Rom. 10:13).[23]

"Jesus' claim to be God caused division among the people. We are not stoning you for any of these miracles,' replied the Jews, 'but for blasphemy, because you, a mere man, claim to be God' (John 10:33). When this apparently ordinary man claimed to be God, and when the title Lord, which meant Yahweh-God to the Jewish mind, was attached to this man Jesus, many rejected Him. If "Lord" when used of Jesus means simply "Sir" or "Master," a term that could have been applied to many others, no one would have been offended. But if "Lord" means that Jesus is Yahweh, that He is the God-Man, the God of the Old Testament manifest in the flesh (John 1:14), then the debate concerning Jesus is understandable. This title of Jesus focuses on His uniqueness. Christ assumed for Himself the title of Lord (Matt. 7:21–22; ...),[24] apparently intending it in the higher

---

[23] Livingston Blauvelt Jr., "Does the Bible Teach Lordship Salvation?," *Bibliotheca Sacra* 143 (1986): 38.

[24] "Not everyone who says to Me, 'Lord, Lord,' will enter the kingdom of heaven; but he who does the will of My Father who is in heaven. ²² Many will say to Me on that day, 'Lord, Lord, did we not prophesy in Your name, and in Your name cast out demons, and in Your name perform many

sense."[25]

Was the charge blasphemy true? The inerrant Text proves otherwise.

On the cross He was the Son of God

Even on the cross He was berated by the public about His person. "He trusts in God; let Him deliver *Him* now, if He takes pleasure in Him; for He said, I am the Son of God, and the robbers also who had been crucified with Him were casting the same insult at Him" (Mat. 27:43-44).

At death He was the Son of God

After His death on the cross there was also the true awareness of His very person by some. "Now the centurion, and those who were with him keeping guard over Jesus, when they saw the earthquake and the things that were happening, became very frightened and said, Truly this was the Son of God!" (Mat. 27:54). "And when the centurion, who was standing right in front of Him, saw the way He breathed His last, he said, truly this man was the Son of God!" (Mark 15:39).

The church's foundation is the Son of God

The entire church age or dispensation is based on one truth and confession and that is Jesus Christ is the Son of God. "Now when Jesus came into the district of Caesarea Philippi, He *began* asking His disciples, saying, Who do people say that the Son of Man is? And they said, some *say* John the Baptist; and others, Elijah; but still others, Jeremiah, or one of the prophets, He said to them, But who do you say that I am? And

---

miracles?" (Mat. 7:21-22);
[25] Livingston Blauvelt Jr., "Does the Bible Teach Lordship Salvation?," *Bibliotheca Sacra* 143 (1986): 39.

Simon Peter answered and said, Thou art the Christ, the Son of the living God. And Jesus answered and said to him, Blessed are you, Simon Barjona, because flesh and blood did not reveal *this* to you, but My Father who is in heaven. And I also say to you that you are Peter, and upon this rock I will build My church; and the gates of Hades shall not overpower it" (Mat. 16:13-18). And this rock was the truth of His very person that Jesus Christ is the Son of God. He is the God-man, literally Jehovah in the flesh. Nothing less than this is biblically the truth concerning His person and true natures i.e. He is the God-man. He is very man of very man and very God of very God. This means He is 100% God and 100% man without admixture of attributes and 100% without sin. He never became 'sin.' He did become the sin offering (2 Cor. 5:21)[26] for all men i.e. the entire human race.

Immediately after Paul's conversion, he began preaching that Jesus is the Son of God. "And Ananias departed and entered the house, and after laying his hands on him said, Brother Saul, the Lord Jesus, who appeared to you on the road by which you were coming, has sent me so that you may regain your sight, and be filled with the Holy Spirit… Now for several days he was with the disciples who were at Damascus, and immediately he *began* to proclaim Jesus in the synagogues, saying, He is the Son of God" (Act 9:17-20).

The essential doctrine of the church age concerns one major teaching. Paul made this very clear. "And He gave some

---

[26] "Paul now summarized the basis of this message. The Cross epitomized the love of God (John 3:16) and of Christ (John 15:13; Rom. 5:8). The Savior was sinless: He **had no sin**. He was "without sin" (Heb. 4:15), and "in Him is no sin" (1 John 3:5). He took on Himself the sin of the world (John 1:29; 1 Peter 2:24; 1 John 2:2). **God made Him … to be sin for us** (cf. Isa. 53:4–6, 10). The sins of the world were placed on Him so that, in turn, His **righteousness** could be given those who trust Him (Rom. 5:17) and are thus **in Him**. That gift of righteousness is obtainable only by faith (Rom. 3:22; 6:23; Eph. 2:8–9; Phil. 3:9)." David K. Lowery, "2 Corinthians," in *The Bible Knowledge Commentary: An Exposition of the Scriptures*, ed. J. F. Walvoord and R. B. Zuck, vol. 2 (Wheaton, IL: Victor Books, 1985), 568.

as apostles, and some *as* prophets, and some *as* evangelists, and some *as* pastors and teachers, for the equipping of the saints for the work of service, to the building up of the body of Christ; until we all attain to the unity of the faith, **and of the knowledge of the Son of God**, to a mature man, to the measure of the stature which belongs to the fullness of Christ" (Eph 4:11-13). The word knowledge is really a full or complete knowledge of the Son of God.[27] "The purpose of the gifted believers (vv. 7–11) is to equip other believers for the ministry so as to give them stability doctrinally and practically and thus lead them to mutual edification… (1) "unto the **unity** of the **faith** (cf. Eph. 4:5) **and** full **knowledge** (*epignōseōs;* cf. 1:17) **of the Son of God**," (2) "unto a **mature** man," and (3) "unto the **measure** (*metron;* cf. 4:7, 16) of the stature **of the fullness of Christ.**"[28] This is not just head knowledge but a true full knowledge that will not only preserve the unity of the faith but stabilize the believing church against false doctrine. Satan's

---

[27] **Till we all attain** (μεχρι καταντησωμεν οἱ παντες [*mechri katantēsōmen hoi pantes*]). Temporal clause with purpose idea with μεχρι [*mechri*] and the first aorist active subjunctive of κατανταω [*katantaō*], late verb, to come down to the goal (Phil. 3:11). "The whole" including every individual. Hence the need of so many gifts. **Unto the unity of the faith** (εἰς την ἑνοτητα της πιστεως [*eis tēn henotēta tēs pisteōs*]). "Unto oneness of faith" (of trust) in Christ (verse 3) which the Gnostics were disturbing. **And of the knowledge of the Son of God** (και της ἐπιγνωσεως του υἱου του θεου [*kai tēs epignōseōs tou huiou tou theou*]). … But Paul adds to this idea "the fulness of Christ" (του πληρωματος του Χριστου [*tou plērōmatos tou Christou*]), like "the fulness of God" in 3:19. And yet some actually profess to be "perfect" with a standard like this to measure by! No pastor has finished his work when the sheep fall so far short of the goal… **That we may be no longer children** (ἱνα μηκετι ὠμεν νηπιοι [*hina mēketi ōmen nēpioi*]). Negative final clause with present subjunctive. Some Christians are quite content to remain "babes" in Christ and never cut their eye-teeth (Heb. 5:11–14), the victims of every charlatan who comes along. A.T. Robertson, *Word Pictures in the New Testament* (Nashville, TN: Broadman Press, 1933), Eph 4:13–14.

[28] Harold W. Hoehner, "Ephesians," in *The Bible Knowledge Commentary: An Exposition of the Scriptures*, ed. J. F. Walvoord and R. B. Zuck, vol. 2 (Wheaton, IL: Victor Books, 1985), 635–636.

primary scheme is to diminish the doctrine of the Person of Jesus Christ i.e. that He is the eternal Son of God, and what He did on the cross. When all this is truly in focus then the results are very clear for believers. "As a result, we are no longer to be children, tossed here and there by waves, and carried about by every wind of doctrine, by the trickery of men, by craftiness in deceitful scheming" (Eph 4:14). Note what was being preached: "For the Son of God, Christ Jesus, who was preached among you by us-- by me and Silvanus and Timothy-- was not yes and no, but is yes in Him" (2 Cor. 1:19). The preaching was about Jesus as the Son of God. The inerrant Text is very clear that the gospel is all about Him.[29]

There are many who have zeal for God but not in accordance with the truth or a full knowledge of Christ. "For I bear them witness that they have a zeal for God, but not in accordance with **knowledge**[30]" (Romans 10:2). "Having stated the fact of Israel's stumbling in the preceding verses, Paul now explained the reason for that stumbling. But first, in words reminiscent of the opening verses of chapter 9, the apostle expressed his deep personal spiritual burden for the salvation of the people of Israel. Perhaps with his own experience in mind (cf. Acts 26:11; Gal. 1:13–14; Phil. 3:4–6) Paul affirmed, **For I can testify** (present tense, "I testify, bear witness") **about them that they are zealous for God**. Israel was called "the God-

---

[29] One must know Who He is and what He did. He is the Eternal Son and He died according to the Scriptures and was raised on the 3rd day according to the Scriptures. Eternal salvation is all according to the Scriptures (1 Cor. 15:1-4) and one must just simply believe.

[30] μαρτυρῶ γὰρ αὐτοῖς ὅτι ζῆλον θεοῦ ἔχουσιν ἀλλ' οὐ κατ' **ἐπίγνωσιν**· ἐπίγνωσις, εως, ἡ κατ' ἐπίγνωσιν in accordance with (real) knowledge Ro 10:2. [30] William Arndt et al., *A Greek-English Lexicon of the New Testament and Other Early Christian Literature :* (Chicago: University of Chicago Press, 1979), 291. [Friberg, *Analytical Greek Lexicon*] ἐπίγνωσις, εως, ἡ knowledge, true knowledge; in the NT of content, used especially of intensive religious and moral knowledge, what one comes to know and appropriate through faith in Christ *(full) knowledge, acknowledgment, recognition* (CO 1.10; 2T 2.25); [Liddell-Scott, *Greek Lexicon*] ἐπίγνωσις, εως, ἡ, (ἐπιγιγνώσκω) *full knowledge*, N.T.

intoxicated people." Paul had to acknowledge, however, that **their zeal is not based on** (lit., "according to") **knowledge** (*epignōsin*, "intensive, full knowledge"). The Jews obviously had knowledge of God but not full knowledge. Otherwise they would not have stumbled over Christ by seeking to gain righteousness on the basis of works."[31]

Schemers and very shallow theology downplay the eternal Sonship of Jesus Christ. The Scriptures are very clear that the expression 'Son of God' when referring to Jesus Christ is a complete declaration of His eternal deity. One must believe that He is the eternal Son of God for that is Who He is! To deny this doctrine is to deny who He is. The inerrant Text is very clear proclaiming this very grand and essential truth about Jesus Christ.

Jesus is the true God and eternally the Son

There are false teachings concerning Jesus especially that He was/is not eternally Jehovah the eternal Son of God. Jesus never became the eternal Son of God, and the Scriptures are totally unambiguous concerning this essential doctrine for salvation i.e. eternal life. "And we know that the Son of God has come, and has given us understanding, in order that we might know Him who is true, and we are in Him who is true, in His Son Jesus Christ. This is the true God and eternal life" (1 John 5:20).[32]

---

[31] John A. Witmer, "Romans," in *The Bible Knowledge Commentary: An Exposition of the Scriptures*, ed. J. F. Walvoord and R. B. Zuck, vol. 2 (Wheaton, IL: Victor Books, 1985), 479.

[32] This One, His Son, His Son Jesus Christ is the true God. The Son has eternally been the true God and the second person of the trinity. **1 John 5:20 And we know that the Son of God has come, and has given us understanding, in order that we might know Him who is true, and we are in Him who is true, in His Son Jesus Christ. This is the true God and eternal life.** οἴδαμεν δὲ ὅτι ὁ υἱὸς τοῦ θεοῦ ἥκει καὶ δέδωκεν ἡμῖν διάνοιαν ἵνα γινώσκωμεν τὸν ἀληθινόν, καὶ ἐσμὲν ἐν τῷ ἀληθινῷ, **ἐν τῷ υἱῷ αὐτοῦ Ἰησοῦ Χριστῷ. οὗτός ἐστιν ὁ ἀληθινὸς θεὸς** καὶ **ζωὴ αἰώνιος.** "Direct

Jesus is the true God and the great God and Savior. "For the grace of God has appeared, bringing salvation to all men, instructing us to deny ungodliness and worldly desires and to live sensibly, righteously and godly in the present age, looking for the blessed hope and the appearing of the glory of our great God and Savior, Christ Jesus" (Titus 2:11-13).[33] Romans 9:5 truly assert Christ's full deity "whose are the fathers, and from whom is the Christ according to the flesh, who is over all, God blessed forever. Amen" (Rom. 9:5).[34] "Also the

---

application is made of the names of God to each of the three Persons. There is no question raised as to the divine titles belonging properly to the Father. Yet the Son and Spirit bear the same designations. The Son is called *God* (John 1:1), *the true God* (1 John 5:20), *the blessed God* (Rom. 9:5), *the great God* (Tit. 2:13). So, also, the Holy Spirit is called *God* (Acts 5:3–9), and *Lord* (2 Cor. 3:18)." Lewis Sperry Chafer, "Trinitarianism," *Bibliotheca Sacra* 97 (1940): 156. "Moreover, the coming of **the Son of God has** granted to believers an **understanding** which makes possible a knowledge of God. John and his circle were **in Him who is true** (and so were his readers as they continued to "abide"). But to abide in God is also to abide **in His Son Jesus Christ**. For that matter, Jesus Christ Himself **is the true God** (cf. John 1:1, 14) **and eternal life** (cf. 1 John 1:2; 2:25; 5:11–13). With this grand affirmation of the deity of Christ, John concluded his summary of apostolic truths which stand against the falsehoods of the antichrists." John F. Walvoord and Roy B. Zuck, Dallas Theological Seminary, *The Bible Knowledge Commentary: An Exposition of the Scriptures*, vol. 2 (Wheaton, IL: Victor Books, 1985), 903–904.

[33] Ἐπεφάνη γὰρ ἡ χάρις τοῦ θεοῦ σωτήριος πᾶσιν ἀνθρώποις ¹² παιδεύουσα ἡμᾶς, ἵνα ἀρνησάμενοι τὴν ἀσέβειαν καὶ τὰς κοσμικὰς ἐπιθυμίας σωφρόνως καὶ δικαίως καὶ εὐσεβῶς ζήσωμεν ἐν τῷ νῦν αἰῶνι, ¹³ προσδεχόμενοι τὴν μακαρίαν ἐλπίδα καὶ ἐπιφάνειαν τῆς δόξης <u>τοῦ</u> **μεγάλου** <u>θεοῦ</u> **καὶ** <u>σωτῆρος</u> <u>ἡμῶν</u> <u>Ἰησοῦ</u> <u>Χριστοῦ</u>.. Note the one article joining both God and savior in one Person i.e. Jesus Christ.

[34] ὧν οἱ πατέρες καὶ ἐξ ὧν **ὁ Χριστὸς** τὸ κατὰ σάρκα, ὁ ὢν ἐπὶ πάντων **θεὸς εὐλογητὸς** εἰς τοὺς αἰῶνας, ἀμήν. (Rom. 9:5) "**Of whom** (ἐξ ὧν [*ex hōn*]). Fourth relative clause and here with ἐξ [*ex*] and the ablative. **Christ** (ὁ Χριστος [*ho Christos*]). The Messiah. **As concerning the flesh** (το κατα σαρκα [*to kata sarka*]). Accusative of general reference, "as to the according to the flesh." Paul limits the descent of Jesus from the Jews to his human side as he did in 1:3f. **Who is over all, God blessed for ever** (ὁ ὢν ἐπι παντων θεος εὐλογητος [*ho on epi pantōn theos eulogētos*]). A clear statement of the deity of Christ following the remark about his humanity."

Israelites were in the line of promise from its beginning in **the patriarchs** (cf. Matt. 1:1–16; Rom. 1:3) to its fulfillment in the Messiah, **who is God over all, forever praised! Amen**. This is a clear affirmation of the deity of Messiah."[35]

The Son was always eternally God the Son and this is why this can be said of Him "Jesus Christ *is* the same yesterday and today, *yes* and forever" (Heb. 13:8). This is not said of any humanity except of the eternal Persons in the eternal Godhead who are eternally immutable.

> "No created thing can be said to be immutable. Jehovah can say of Himself, "I am the LORD ['Jehovah'], I change not" (Mal. 3:6). Psalm 102:25–27 is a message concerning Jehovah which is quoted in Hebrews 1:10–12, and there applied to Christ, and after this manner, "Thou, Lord, in the beginning hast laid the foundation of the earth; and the heavens are the works of thine hands: they shall perish; but thou remainest; and they all shall wax old as doth a garment; and as a vesture shalt thou fold them up, and they shall be changed: but thou art the same, and thy years shall not fail." The Lord Jesus Christ is "the same yesterday, and today, and forever" (Heb. 13:8)."[36]

Jesus as the eternal Son could not change in person, position, attributes, etc. for these attributes or eternal capacities are eternally immutable within the Godhead. The Father is eternally God the Father, the Holy Spirit is eternally God the Holy Spirit, and the Son is eternally God the Son.[37] The Scriptures are very clear that the Father is Jehovah, the Son is Jehovah, and the Holy Spirit is Jehovah. All three persons of

---

A.T. Robertson, *Word Pictures in the New Testament* (Nashville, TN: Broadman Press, 1933), Ro 9:5.

[35] John A. Witmer, "Romans," in *The Bible Knowledge Commentary: An Exposition of the Scriptures*, ed. J. F. Walvoord and R. B. Zuck, vol. 2 (Wheaton, IL: Victor Books, 1985), 476.

[36] Lewis Sperry Chafer, *Systematic Theology*, vol. 1 (Grand Rapids, MI: Kregel Publications, 1993), 341.

[37] The three Persons of the triune Godhead are immutable i.e. change is not possible.

the Godhead are omnipresent, omniscient, and omnipotent. All three persons of the Godhead are coequal, coeternal, and coessential. There is one God existing eternally in three distinct persons, but the unity is that there is one God.

> "When we have approached the doctrine by means of the personal experience of redemption, we are prepared to give full consideration to the two lines of teaching found in the New Testament. (a) One line of teaching insists on the unity of the Godhead (1 Cor. 8:4; James 2:19); and (b) the other reveals distinctions within the Godhead (Matt. 3:16, 17; 28:19; 2 Cor. 13:14). We see clearly that (1) the Father is God (Matt. 11:25; Rom. 15:6; Eph. 4:6); (2) the Son is God (John 1:1, 18; 20:28; Acts 20:28; Rom. 9:5; Heb. 1:8; Col. 2:9; Phil. 2:6; 2 Pet. 1:1); (3) the Holy Spirit is God (Acts 5:3, 4; 1 Cor. 2:10, 11; Eph. 2:22); (4) the Father, Son, and Holy Spirit are distinct from one another, sending and being sent, honouring and being honoured. The Father honours the Son, the Son honours the Father, and the Holy Spirit honours the Son (John 15:26; 16:13, 14; 17:1, 8, 18, 23)… We see this very clearly in Heb. 10:7–17, where the Father wills, the Son works and the Spirit witnesses. The elements of the plan of redemption thus find their root, foundation, and spring in the nature of the Godhead; and the obvious reason why these distinctions which we express by the terms "Person" and "Trinity" were not revealed earlier than New Testament times is that not until then was redemption accomplished."[38]

"Not that any man has seen the Father, except the One who is from God; He has seen the Father" (John 6:46); "Jesus said to him, Have I been so long with you, and *yet* you have not come to know Me, Philip? He who has seen Me has seen the Father; how do you say, Show us the Father?" (John 14:9). All the Father is, is in the Son, and all the Son is, is in the Father. As the Godhead is immutable, the Father Son relationship has been eternal. "For in Him all the fulness of Deity dwells in bodily form." (Col. 2:9)

---

[38] Lewis Sperry Chafer, *Systematic Theology*, vol. 6 (Grand Rapids, MI: Kregel Publications, 1993), 8–9.

False teaching concerning the eternal Son

There are those who are rather cavalier in their assessment of the triune Godhead especially concerning eternal attributes. They try to prove the Father Son relationship within the Godhead was not eternal. Again, this shows a rather superficial view of the Scriptures and what is being taught.

Jesus is the eternal Son of God who never changes for He is the same forever and ever (Heb. 13:8). The Father called His Son God,[39] and when one confesses this, he/she is simply agreeing with the Father that Jesus is LORD.

When one believes or confesses that Jesus is LORD, he is agreeing with what the inerrant Word has revealed. Jesus is LORD in the true sense that He is the true Jehovah God. One must believe He is the Son of God=Jehovah for that is who He is eternally. Scripture is very clear with this doctrine.

When anyone confesses Jesus is LORD, he is saying Jesus is the eternal Son of God for the Son of God is LORD and Creator of all the ages which includes the entire universe (Heb. 1:2, 11:3). God the Father, God the Son, and God the Holy Spirit were involved in the creation, but the eternal Son was the prime Agent of the creation (John 1:3; Col. 1:16).[40] All things were created by and for the Eternal Son. (There will be much

---

[39] "But of the Son *He says*, Thy throne, O God, is forever and ever, And the righteous scepter is the scepter of His kingdom… And, Thou, Lord, in the beginning didst lay the foundation of the earth, And the heavens are the works of Thy hands; They will perish, but Thou **remainest**; **And they all will become old as a garment**, And as a mantle Thou wilt roll them up; As a garment they will also be changed. **But Thou art the same, and Thy years will not come to an end**" (Heb. 1:8-12). God's Word proves the Son to be eternally unchangeable, for He is God, He is the eternal Son of God.

[40] "All things came into being by Him, and apart from Him nothing came into being that has come into being" (John 1:3); "For by Him all things were created, *both* in the heavens and on earth, visible and invisible, whether thrones or dominions or rulers or authorities-- all things have been created by Him and for Him" (Col. 1:16).

more concerning this doctrine in chapter 3)

The Father called His Son God

The Father called His Son God. It must be kept in focus that the Son of God is coeternal, coequal, and coessential with the Father.[41] "But of the Son *He says*, Thy throne, O God, is forever and ever, and the righteous scepter is the scepter of His kingdom" (Heb 1:8).[42] Note the context of this passage.

> "But of the **Son** *He says*, Thy throne, **O God**, is forever and ever, And the righteous scepter is the scepter of His kingdom. Thou hast loved righteousness and hated lawlessness; Therefore God, Thy God, hath anointed Thee with the oil of gladness above Thy companions. **And, Thou, Lord, in the beginning didst lay the foundation of the earth, And the heavens are the works of Thy hands; They will perish, but Thou remainest; And they all will become old as a garment, And as a mantle Thou wilt roll them up; As a garment they will also be changed**. **But Thou art the same, And Thy years will not come to an end. But to which of the angels has He ever said, Sit at My right hand, Until I make Thine enemies A footstool for Thy feet**?" (Heb 1:8-13).

The writer is quoting Psalm 102. "Of old Thou didst found the earth; and the heavens are the work of Thy hands. Even

---

[41] He did not become the Son of God for He was eternally the Son of God, He was/is immutable as the entire Godhead.

[42] 1:7–9. In a pair of contrasting quotations, the author juxtaposed the servanthood of **the angels** (v. 7) and the eternal dominion of **the Son** (vv. 8–9). It is possible that, in line with one strand of Jewish thought about angels (cf. 2 Esdras 8:21–22), the writer understood the statement of Psalm 104:4 (quoted in Heb. 1:7) as suggesting that angels often blended their mutable natures with **winds** or **fire** as they performed the tasks God gave them. But in contrast with this mutability, the Son's **throne** is eternal and immutable (v. 8). Zane C. Hodges, "Hebrews," in *The Bible Knowledge Commentary: An Exposition of the Scriptures*, ed. J. F. Walvoord and R. B. Zuck, vol. 2 (Wheaton, IL: Victor Books, 1985), 782.

they will perish, but Thou dost endure; and all of them will wear out like a garment; like clothing Thou wilt change them, and they will be changed. But Thou art the same, and Thy years will not come to an end" (Psalm 102:25-27). This is proving Jesus is the Creator as the Son of God who can never change. He is immutable as the Son for He is Jehovah the Son of God and cannot change in any attribute or manner. "Speaking of God's eternality in contrast with His Creation was an expression of the psalmist's confidence in the Lord. **The earth and the heavens will perish** (cf. 2 Peter 3:10; Rev. 21:1), wearing **out like** old clothes. By contrast God is unchanging (Mal. 3:6; Heb. 13:8) and eternal (His **years will never end**; cf. Ps. 102:27). Therefore He will be faithful to all generations (to the saints' **children** and to **their descendants**). Verses 25–27 are applied to Christ in Hebrews 1:10–12. The psalmist was addressing the eternal Lord, and the writer of Hebrews identified Jesus Christ as the eternal One, the Creator and Sustainer of the world. This is a strong affirmation of the deity of Jesus Christ."[43]

Jesus Christ is the eternal one. He is the eternal Son and the Text is completely clear with this truth. The Father is Jehovah God, the Son is Jehovah God, and the Holy Spirit is Jehovah God. All three persons in the Godhead are distinct persons yet within perfect unity of the Godhead.

> "One line of teaching insists on the unity of the Godhead (1 Cor. 8:4; James 2:19); and (b) the other reveals distinctions within the Godhead (Matt. 3:16, 17; 28:19; 2 Cor. 13:14). We see clearly that (1) the Father is God (Matt. 11:25; Rom. 15:6; Eph. 4:6); (2) the Son is God (John 1:1, 18; 20:28; Acts 20:28; Rom. 9:5; Heb. 1:8; Col. 2:9; Phil. 2:6; 2 Pet. 1:1); (3) the Holy Spirit is God (Acts 5:3, 4; 1 Cor. 2:10, 11; Eph. 2:22);

---

[43] Allen P. Ross, "Psalms," in *The Bible Knowledge Commentary: An Exposition of the Scriptures*, ed. J. F. Walvoord and R. B. Zuck, vol. 1 (Wheaton, IL: Victor Books, 1985), 867.

(4) the Father, Son, and Holy Spirit are distinct from one another, sending and being sent, honouring and being honoured. The Father honours the Son, the Son honours the Father, and the Holy Spirit honours the Son (John 15:26; 16:13, 14; 17:1, 8, 18, 23)."[44]

Anyone who simply believes on Him that is Who He is and what He did has eternal life (John 3:16). "And after he brought them out, he said, Sirs, what must I do to be saved? And they said, Believe in the Lord Jesus, and you shall be saved, you and your household" (Acts 16:30-31).[45] It must be continually reminded that believing on Him is believing or trusting in all that the Father has revealed concerning the Son in all His Word. To deny what the Word has revealed concerning the Son of God is the same as not believing. When one 'confesses' Christ biblically, he/she is agreeing with what God has revealed especially concerning the Son of God i.e. who He is and what He did. This includes His Person, His life, His works, His death, and His resurrection. The only way anyone could know he/she has eternal life is by His inerrant Word. "These things I have written to you who believe in the name of the Son of God, in order that you may know that you have eternal life" (1 John 5:13). Satan knows this very well and Christ Himself was very clear with this especially in certain parables. "Now the parable is this: the seed is the word of God, and those beside the road are those who have heard; then the devil comes and takes away the word from their heart, so that they may not believe and be saved" (Luke 8:11-12).

Again, one must believe who He is and what He did. Jesus as the eternal Son of God is the only true bread of eternal

---

[44] Lewis Sperry Chafer, *Systematic Theology*, vol. 6 (Grand Rapids, MI: Kregel Publications, 1993), 8.
[45] Believe in the Lord Jesus is saying 'believe in the LORD Jesus, for Jesus is LORD.'

life.[46] No one can come to the eternal Father except by the eternal Son of God. "Truly, truly, I say to you, an hour is coming and now is, when the dead shall hear the voice of the Son of God; and those who hear shall live" (John 5:25). "Let not your heart be troubled; believe in God, believe also in Me. In My Father's house are many dwelling places; if it were not so, I would have told you; for I go to prepare a place for you. And if I go and prepare a place for you, I will come again, and receive you to Myself; that where I am, *there* you may be also. And you know the way where I am going. Thomas said to Him, Lord, we do not know where You are going, how do we know the way? Jesus said to him, **I am the way, and the truth, and the life; no one comes to the Father, but through Me.** If you had known Me, you would have known My Father also; from now on you know Him, and have seen Him" (John 14:1-7). Again, the only way to the Father is by the eternal Son.

Conclusion

The designation Son of God applied to Christ means eternal deity

Jesus was on trial for being the Son of God. That is the true charge against Him. This is quite obvious and actually begins very early in the ministry of Christ. "For this cause

---

[46] The Jews therefore were grumbling about Him, because He said, "I am the bread that came down out of heaven." [42] And they were saying, "Is not this Jesus, the son of Joseph, whose father and mother we know? How does He now say, 'I have come down out of heaven'?" [43] Jesus answered and said to them, "Do not grumble among yourselves. [44] "No one can come to Me, unless the Father who sent Me draws him; and I will raise him up on the last day. [45] "It is written in the prophets, 'And they shall all be taught of God.' Everyone who has heard and learned from the Father, comes to Me. [46] "Not that any man has seen the Father, except the One who is from God; He has seen the Father. [47] "Truly, truly, I say to you, he who believes has eternal life. [48] "I am the bread of life" (John 6:41-48).

therefore the Jews were seeking all the more to kill Him, because He not only was breaking the Sabbath, but also was calling God His own Father, making Himself equal with God" (John 5:18).

"John's Gospel makes much of the Son of God title and properly, since it is the Gospel of His Deity. In that Gospel, *the Son*—which evidently is an abbreviation of the full title *the Son of God*—executes judgment (5:22); He has life in Himself and quickeneth whom He will (5:26, 21). He gives eternal life (10:10); it is the will of the Father that all men should honor the Son, even as they honor the Father (5:23); the Son does only what He sees the Father do (5:19), and only that which He hears from the Father does He speak (14:10); and the Son confesses that, on the divine side, He has a Father and on the human side He has a God (20:17). A conclusive and arresting Scripture in this connection is Matthew 28:18–20, which reads: "And Jesus came and spake unto them, saying, All power is given unto me in heaven and in earth. Go ye therefore, and teach all nations, baptizing them in the name of the Father, and of the Son, and of the Holy Ghost: teaching them to observe all things whatsoever I have commanded you: and, lo, I am with you always, even unto the end of the world. Amen." Here it is seen that not only all authority is given to the Son, but He is named in the Trinity on an equality with the other Persons of the Godhead."[47] "It follows that if Christ is God then He has existed from all eternity. Evidence that He is God may be seen in His titles—Logos, Only Begotten, Express Image, First Begotten, Elohim, and Jehovah; in His divine attributes—eternity (Mic. 5:2), immutability (Heb. 1:11–12; 13:8), omnipotence (1 Cor. 15:28; Phil. 3:21), omniscience, and omnipresence; in His mighty works—creation, preservation, forgiveness of sin, raising the dead, and execution of all judgment."[48] "The Incarnation means

---

[47] Lewis Sperry Chafer, "Trinitarianism," *Bibliotheca Sacra* 97 (1940): 394–396.
[48] Lewis Sperry Chafer, *Systematic Theology* (Grand Rapids, MI: Kregel Publications, 1993), 78.

that the eternal Son of God became human in the Person of Jesus Christ. But it also means that God came to communicate to humankind within culture. Not only did the Word become flesh, but also the Word made His dwelling among us (John 1:14). In the Incarnation God came in human flesh, but He also came into a human culture."[49]

> "He who believes in Him is not judged; he who does not believe has been judged already, because he has not believed in the name of the only begotten Son of God" (John 3:18)[50]

---

[49] Leith Anderson, "Theological Issues of 21st-Century Ministry," *Bibliotheca Sacra* 151 (1994): 134.

[50] ὁ πιστεύων εἰς αὐτὸν οὐ κρίνεται· ὁ δὲ μὴ πιστεύων ἤδη κέκριται, ὅτι μὴ πεπίστευκεν εἰς τὸ ὄνομα τοῦ **μονογενοῦς** υἱοῦ τοῦ θεοῦ. **μονογενής, ές** ... **pertaining to being the only one of its kind or class, *unique (in kind)*** of something that is the only example of its category ... τὸν υἱὸν τὸν μ. ἔδωκεν **J 3:16** ... ὁ μ. υἱὸς τοῦ θεοῦ vs. **18**; τὸν υἱὸν τὸν μ. ἀπέσταλκεν ὁ θεός **1J 4:9**; William Arndt, Frederick W. Danker, and Walter Bauer, *A Greek-English Lexicon of the New Testament and Other Early Christian Literature* (Chicago: University of Chicago Press, 2000), 658.

His Creation, the Angels, the Sons of God

Man was created in the image of God. Man is both immaterial and material what some call body and soul or spirit. His material part was created from dust but his immaterial part was not created but breathed into man by God and he became a living being. "Then the LORD God formed **man of dust from the ground**, and breathed into his nostrils the breath of life; and man **became a living being**" (Gen 2:7). "It is clear, however, that the immaterial part of man originates not as a creation, but as a transmission. Some element of creation may have been present and active, but it is evident that the "living soul" which man became by the divine inbreathing is more uncreated than created. It is an impartation from the Eternal One. Angels are created beings (Col. 1:16), and, since they are immaterial, it follows that their beings, in all their features, are a direct creation quite apart from preexisting matter."[1]

It must be continually observed that *all* the angelic beings are created and their abode is heaven not earth. They are active in both earth and heaven as recorded in the Text, and it is essential to understand that all angels are creatures. "The angels are created beings (Ps. 148:2–5; Col. 1:16), their abode is in heaven (Matt. 24:36), their activity is both on earth and in heaven (Ps. 103:20; Luke 15:10; Heb. 1:14), and their destiny is in the celestial city (Heb. 12:22; Rev. 21:12). They remain angels throughout their existence, they neither propagate nor do they die. There is no reason for confusing the angels with any other creatures of God's universe. Even though they fall, as in the case of Satan and the demons, they are still classed as angels (Matt. 25:41)".[2]

There is so much misinformation concerning angels and their ability/ies to somehow transform their immaterial being/s

---

[1] Lewis Sperry Chafer, *Systematic Theology*, vol. 2 (Grand Rapids, MI: Kregel Publications, 1993), 160–161.
[2] Lewis Sperry Chafer, *Systematic Theology*, vol. 1 (Grand Rapids, MI: Kregel Publications, 1993), 37.

into material and even cohabit with woman. There is much information which can be presented which is extra biblical but a believer's source for all faith and practice is the inerrant Word of God.

This chapter addresses much information about angels especially did angels ever cohabit? Are the sons of God angelic beings in Gen. 6:1-4? Who are the sons of God? Can evil angels be sons of God? Is Satan a son of God? And several other associated issues will be addressed. (Please see Appendix F for more information concerning 'the sons of God and Satan.')

Some information presented in this chapter will be repeated from other chapters directly associated with His creation. This is essential as the context must be kept in focus concerning the Creator and the creatures.

Did angels cohabit?
(Gen. 6:1-4; 2 Peter 2:4; Jude 1:6-7)

The issue

There has been much biblical controversy concerning angels[3] being able to cohabit with women. This argument is normally in association with Genesis 6:1-4, 2 Peter 2:4, and Jude 1:6-7. There are other verses but these are the primary verses that will be addressed. It is noted that many biblically conservative commentators and scholars have held to the position of angelic cohabitation (Gen. 6:1-4). While there may be differences within these views, one predominant view seems to be that angels did cohabit in Gen. 6:1-4 and produce an offspring.

The two primary passages that will be presented concerning the possibility of angelic cohabitation are Gen 6:1-4 and Jude 1:6-7. It is not this writer's purpose to present various views, but to present a contextual yet simple option for these verses.

---

[3] angelic beings

Since all Scripture is God breathed which means all Scripture originates with Him and Him alone then all Text is inerrant for God cannot err. Interpretation must be based on a literal, grammatical, and historical hermeneutic and not based on a theological interpretation. Primary interpretation must begin and end with context, context, and then context.

Gen. 6:1-4

Context of Gen. 6:1-4

Genesis begins with God as the Creator of everything and His creation as we know it biblically. He is the Author and Finisher of all creation and has revealed to man exactly what He did. From Genesis 1:1 to Revelation 22:21 God, as the Creator, has made it exceptionally clear what He wants man to know about Him and His creation. To read more into the Text than the Text has revealed is eisogesis and mere speculation.[4]

As this has already been addressed Genesis 1:1 – 2:25 is the biblical record of beginnings primarily for the creation of the heavens and the earth, man and man's habitation i.e. the earth. Genesis records nine beginnings and ten family histories.[5] The earth, as revealed in the Text, was created to be inhabited by man.[6]

The earth was formless and void תֹהוּ וָבֹהוּ (*tohu*

---

[4] He included the exact details He wants all men to know and understand.
[5] Beginnings: Gen. 1:1; 2:4; 3:1; 3:8; 4:1; 4:16; 10:1; 11:1; 11:10; family histories: 1:1; 5:1; 6:9; 10:1; 11:10; 11:27; 25:12; 25:19; 36:1; 37:2.
[6] The earth was created to be inhabited by man and ruled over by man. "For thus says the LORD, who created the heavens (He is the God who formed the earth and made it, He established it and did not create it a waste place, *But* formed it to be inhabited), "I am the LORD, and there is none else" (Isa. 45:18); "What is man, that Thou dost take thought of him? And the son of man, that Thou dost care for him? [5] Yet Thou hast made him a little lower than God, And dost crown him with glory and majesty! [6] Thou dost make him to rule over the works of Thy hands; Thou hast put all things under his feet" (Ps. 8:4).

wabohu) was simply the creation's primordial state.[7] (Please see Appendix B) There was primordial substance[8] and He formed it into what He wanted out of water by water as the Creator.[9] In essence Jesus is the Creator of all things even the angelic world.

"All things came into being by Him, and apart from Him nothing came into being that has come into being. (John 1:3); "For by Him all things were created, *both* in the heavens and on earth, visible and invisible, whether thrones or dominions or rulers or authorities-- <u>all things have been created by Him and for Him</u>" (Col. 1:16). Again, as this has already been discussed there is absolutely nothing in the Text especially the context of Genesis 1:1-2 indicating there was a previous creation or multiple creations other than the one He has revealed to man.[10] All things of His creation have been created by Him and for Him.[11] If He had destroyed a previous creation or perhaps a

---

[7] Some excellent commentators use the expression unformed and unfilled which is very biblical.

[8] תֹּהוּ *tōhû* ... n.m. ... formlessness, confusion, unreality, emptiness (primary meaning difficult to seize; (old versions) usually κενόν, οὐδέν, μάταιον, *inane, vacuum, vanum;* ...—**1. *formlessness*, of primaeval earth Gn 1:2** ... Francis Brown, Samuel Rolles Driver, and Charles Augustus Briggs, *Enhanced Brown-Driver-Briggs Hebrew and English Lexicon* (Oxford: Clarendon Press, 1977), 1062.

בֹּהוּ *bōhû* ... n. m. **emptiness** ... always with תֹּהוּ *quod vide* תֹּהוּ וָבֹהוּ **Gn 1:2 of primæval earth;** Francis Brown, Samuel Rolles Driver, and Charles Augustus Briggs, *Enhanced Brown-Driver-Briggs Hebrew and English Lexicon* (Oxford: Clarendon Press, 1977), 96.

[9] "Then God said, "Let there be an expanse in the midst of the waters, and let it separate the waters from the waters" (Gen. 1:6); 'Then God said, "Let the waters below the heavens be gathered into one place, and let the dry land appear"; and it was so" (Gen. 1:9); "For when they maintain this, it escapes their notice that by the word of God *the* heavens existed long ago and *the* earth was formed out of water and by water" (2 Pet. 3:5).

[10] This has been previously discussed in chapter 3, yet so essential to recap in context.

[11] "For by Him all things were created, *both* in the heavens and on earth, visible and invisible, whether thrones or dominions or rulers or authorities--

previous earth, it appears it would be very clear in the Text. God had predicted future destructions such as Sodom and Gomorrah and even the flood. God is very clear about all the global and heavenly purging during 'the day of the Lord' which is major biblical doctrine.[12] He is very clear about the new heavens and the new earth when the present system passes away i.e. He literally destroys the present heavens and earth in the day of the Lord.[13] If the Lord destroyed a past heaven and earth or just any earth, it seems it would be in the Text for man to know and fully understand. However, God never intended His Word to be a guessing game, especially with so many divergent views of creation which seem to grow on a daily basis.

Everything God wants us to know is spelled out clearly in and by His Word, so there is no room for speculation.[14] If one 'speculates,' then it should be made clear of the speculation or theory. The Lord created the earth to be inhabited, He did

---

all things have been created by Him and for Him" (Col. 1:16). All things have been created by Him and for Him and definitely not for angels. Angels are created beings and created by Him and for Him as all this creation not some past creation. Angels were never given dominion over any creation as man was given over this creation. There is no defined kingdom program or covenanted program as there is with man. There is so much information and speculation read into the Text concerning creation, it is almost impossible to present all the views and make sense out of them especially by what is presented in His Word.

[12] The church is removed prior to the day of the Lord. Please reference this author's 'The Greatness of the Rapture, The Pre-day of the Lord Rapture.'

[13] "But the day of the Lord will come like a thief, in **which the heavens will pass away with a roar and the elements will be destroyed with intense heat, and the earth and its works will be burned up.** [11] Since all these things are to be destroyed in this way, what sort of people ought you to be in holy conduct and godliness, [12] looking for and hastening the coming of the day of God, **on account of which the heavens will be destroyed by burning, and the elements will melt with intense heat!** [13] But according to His promise we are looking for new heavens and a new earth, in which righteousness dwells. [14] Therefore, beloved, since you look for these things, be diligent to be found by Him in peace, spotless and blameless" (2 Peter 3:10-14).

[14] There is always the habit of reading so much into any given Text when the simplicity of truth is usually so simple.

not create it empty or in vain. "For thus says the LORD, who created the heavens (He is the God who formed the earth and made it, He established it and did not create it a waste place, *But formed it to be inhabited*), I am the LORD, and there is none else" Isaiah:18).[15] The word for 'waste place' is תֹהוּ [16] which can be translated 'in vain' or 'empty' as several translators or translations have done and even the LXX.[17]

---

[15] כִּי כֹה אָמַר־יְהוָה בּוֹרֵא הַשָּׁמַיִם הוּא הָאֱלֹהִים יֹצֵר הָאָרֶץ וְעֹשָׂהּ הוּא כוֹנְנָהּ **לֹא־תֹהוּ** בְרָאָהּ לָשֶׁבֶת יְצָרָהּ אֲנִי יְהוָה וְאֵין עוֹד׃

[16] תֹהוּ formlessness, confusion, unreality, emptiness (primary meaning difficult to seize; old versions usually κενόν, μάταιον, *inane, vacuum, vanum;* ...**1.** *formlessness*, of primaeval earth Gen. 1:2. Francis Brown, Samuel Rolles Driver and Charles Augustus Briggs, *Enhanced Brown-Driver-Briggs Hebrew and English Lexicon* (Oxford: Clarendon Press, 1977), 1062.

[17] The following versions translate Is.45:18 as follows:. "For this is what the LORD says-- God is the Creator of the heavens. He formed the earth and made it. He established it; He did not create it to be **empty**, but formed it to be inhabited-- "I am the LORD, and there is no other" (Common English Bible). "For thus saith the Lord that created the heavens, God himself that formed the earth, and made it, the very maker thereof: he did not create it **in vain**: he formed it to be inhabited. I am the Lord, and there is no other" (Douay-Rheims American Edition, 1899). "For thus says the LORD, who created the heavens (he is God!), who formed the earth and made it (he established it; he did not create it **empty**, he formed it to be inhabited!): "I am the LORD, and there is no other" (English Standard Version, 2007 update). "For thus saith the Lord (that created heauen, God himselfe, that formed the earth, and made it: he that prepared it, he created it not in **vaine**: he formed it to be inhabited) I am the Lord, and there is none other" (Geneva Bible, 1599). "For thus saith the LORD that created the heavens; God himself that formed the earth and made it; he hath established it, he created it not **in vain**, he formed it to be inhabited: I *am* the LORD; and *there is* none else" (King James). "For this is what the LORD says-- he who created the heavens, he is God; he who fashioned and made the earth, he founded it; he did not create it to be **empty**, but formed it to be inhabited-- he says: "I am the LORD, and there is no other" (New International Version). "For thus says the LORD, Who created the heavens, Who is God, Who formed the earth and made it, Who has established it, Who did not create it **in vain**, Who formed it to be inhabited: "I *am* the LORD, and *there is* no other" (New King James Version, 1982). "For thus said Jehovah, Creator of heaven, He is God, Former of earth, and its Maker, He established it -- not **empty** He prepared it, For inhabiting He formed it: 'I *am* Jehovah, and there is none else" (Young's Literal Translation, 1862/1898). "οὕτως λέγει κύριος ὁ ποιήσας τὸν οὐρανόν οὗτος ὁ θεὸς ὁ καταδείξας τὴν γῆν καὶ ποιήσας αὐτήν αὐτὸς διώρισεν αὐτήν οὐκ **εἰς κενόν**[17] ἐποίησεν αὐτὴν ἀλλὰ κατοικεῖσθαι ἐγώ εἰμι καὶ οὐκ ἔστιν ἔτι" (LXX, Septuaginta Ralfhs'). 'In vain, or empty' would be the norm

Man was created in the image of God not only for fellowship with his Creator, but to rule under or with God over the earth (man's habitation) which He created for man.[18] But man chose willfully to rebel against His Creator. "And He said, "Who told you that you were naked? Have you eaten from the tree of which I commanded you not to eat?" (Gen 3:11). Man with his free will chose against God and fell into condemnation.[19]

In light of man's fall into sin, God immediately made one of the greatest promises in the Text. "And I will put enmity between you and the woman, and between your seed and her seed; He shall bruise you on the head, and you shall bruise him on the heel" (Gen. 3:15). All men were to look for this coming promised seed who would bruise or crush (which is a better meaning) the serpent i.e. Satan (Gen. 3:14; Rev. 20:2).

The godless line and the Godly line

Genesis 4:1-15 tells the sad truth of Cain and the murder of Abel. Genesis 4:16-24 gives the miserable state of Cain and his godless genealogy. Genesis 4:25-5:32 presents the birth of Seth and his Godly genealogy especially that of Noah. It is so important to keep in focus that the Lord was establishing His godly line especially that of the promised seed (Gen. 3:15).[20]

---

from the LXX.

[18] Genesis records the beginning of the human race. There is only one race created by God and this race is human. Yet God breathed into man/Adam and he became a living soul in God's image. "Then God said, "Let Us make man in Our image,[18] according to Our likeness; and let them rule over the fish of the sea and over the birds of the sky and over the cattle and over all the earth, and over every creeping thing that creeps on the earth" (Gen. 1:26). Please see Appendix B.

[19]"**So then as through one transgression there resulted condemnation to all men,** even so through one act of righteousness there resulted justification of life to all men" (Rom. 5:19).

[20] One must keep the Godly seed line in focus. This seed line can be traced from Mary back to Adam (Luke 3:23-38). God established a godly line through which the promised seed would come (Gen. 3:15).

"And Adam had relations with his wife again; and she gave birth to a son, and named him Seth, for, *she said*, 'God has appointed me another offspring in place of Abel; for Cain killed him.' And to Seth, to him also a son was born; and he called his name Enosh. Then *men* began to call upon the name of the LORD" (Gen. 4:25-26). Until the birth of Seth and then his son Enosh, the history of man was in essence totally godless. "In strong contrast with this godless society were the righteous. In the line from **Seth** there was faith. **Seth** himself was a provision from **God**, according to Eve's statement of faith. In the days of **Enosh**, Seth's son, **men began to call on** (better, "proclaim") **the name of the LORD** (*Yahweh*)."[21] A Godly line of men from Adam and Eve began with their son Seth. From this Godly line came Lamech and then Noah.

"And Lamech lived one hundred and eighty-two years, and became the father of a son.[29] Now he called his name Noah, saying, "This one shall give us rest from our work and from the toil of our hands *arising* from the ground which the LORD has cursed" (Gen. 5:28-29).

Noah was a genuine light in a world of complete evil and ungodly men. "These are *the records of* the generations of Noah. Noah was a righteous man, blameless in his time; Noah walked with God" (Gen 6:9). Context places Genesis 6 after the birth and genealogy of the line of Seth until Noah and his sons (Gen. 4:25-5:32).[22] "And Noah was five hundred years old, and

---

[21] Allen P. Ross, "Genesis" In , in *The Bible Knowledge Commentary: An Exposition of the Scriptures*, ed. J. F. Walvoord and R. B. Zuck (Wheaton, IL: Victor Books, 1985), Gen. 4:25–26.

[22] "This is the book of the generations of Adam. In the day when God created man, He made him in the likeness of God. ² He created them male and female, and He blessed them and named them Man in the day when they were created. ³ When Adam had lived one hundred and thirty years, he became the father of *a son* in his own likeness, according to his image, and named him **Seth**. ⁴ Then the days of Adam after he became the father of **Seth** were eight hundred years, and he had *other* sons and daughters. ⁵ So all the days that Adam lived were nine hundred and thirty years, and he died. ⁶ And **Seth** lived one hundred and five years, and became the father of Enosh. ⁷ Then **Seth** lived eight hundred and seven years after he became the father of

Noah became the father of Shem, Ham, and Japheth" (Gen. 5:32). God preserved His godly line of men which could easily be called sons of God. Again, the most important issue stems from the promised seed (Gen. 3:15) which would come against that of an ungodly line or ungodly sons. God would preserve His godly seed line.[23]

Gen. 6:1-4

"Now it came about, when men began to multiply on the face of the land, and daughters were born to them, ² that the **sons of God** saw that the daughters of men were beautiful; and they took wives for themselves, whomever they chose. ³ Then the LORD said, "My Spirit shall not strive with man forever, because he also is flesh; nevertheless his days shall be one hundred and twenty years." ⁴ The Nephilim were on the earth in those days, and also afterward, when the **sons of God** came in to the daughters of men, and they bore *children* to them. Those were the mighty men who *were* of old, men of renown" (Gen. 6:1-4).

The first observation is that men began to multiply on the face of the earth (6:1). Verse two states that the **sons of God** saw the daughters of men and took them as wives. When the **sons of God** had relations with the daughters of men, they bore children. There is absolutely nothing in the context up to verse 6 which leads to anything other than these are **sons of God**. Sons of God in context mean that they are of God and they are His. There is nothing novel here in the context.

These children of this relationship became mighty men who were of renown or 'had a name or wanted a/the name' (6:4). The Hebrew construction here is merely הַשֵּׁם 'hashem'

Enosh, and he had *other* sons and daughters. ⁸ So all the days of **Seth** were nine hundred and twelve years, and he died. (Gen. 5:1-8).

[23] This can easily be and proven in Luke 3 with Mary's genealogy back to Adam (Luke 3:23-38). Note the name's included from the Godly line in Genesis 4:26 -5:32.

literally 'the name' or reputation and with the construct 'the men of the name'.[24] They wanted a name for themselves absolutely and completely without God not His name. This line became more and more corrupt as there is even no mention of God in any sense for it is a truly godless line. The world independent of God exalts itself not God. The world likes to hear about the glory of man not its Creator. Man who has departed from God will exalt mankind and his hatred of God simply grows and grows. This is easily understood not only here but in the history of the human race.

These are human children/men by the biblical norm that are born in Adam and nothing here in context to contradict that. All men are in Adam. If this union were of angels they would no longer be men especially men in Adam. Angels are nowhere to be found in this context except by all forms of eisogeting the Text.

The reason for the flood

The Lord made it very clear why He was bringing judgment on the earth. "Then the LORD saw that the wickedness of man was great on the earth, and that every intent of the thoughts of his heart was only evil continually" (Gen. 6:5).[25]

Then the LORD saw that:
1.   the **wickedness** of man was **great** on **the earth**, and
2.   that **every intent** of the thoughts of his heart **was only evil** continually (Gen. 6:5)

---

[24] וְגַם אַחֲרֵי־כֵן אֲשֶׁר יָבֹאוּ בְּנֵי הָאֱלֹהִים אֶל־בְּנוֹת הָאָדָם וְיָלְדוּ לָהֶם הֵמָּה הַגִּבֹּרִים אֲשֶׁר מֵעוֹלָם **אַנְשֵׁי הַשֵּׁם**:
Literally 'the men of the name'

[25] וַיַּרְא יְהוָה כִּי רַבָּה רָעַת הָאָדָם בָּאָרֶץ וְכָל־יֵצֶר מַחְשְׁבֹת לִבּוֹ **רַק רַע כָּל־הַיּוֹם**: Literally 'only evil all the day, always'

This past judgment of God (the flood) was because men were continually consumed by wickedness and nothing else. Men only wanted to do evil at every moment. The saying at that time might have been 'let's do evil 24/7'. The only thing on man's heart was not only to do evil but to do more and more evil.[26] Man was so consumed by the pleasure/s of evil there was absolutely nothing else in his being.

The Lord did not want to bring judgment (the flood)

Because of the continued wickedness of all men, the Lord grieved to bring a total judgment on the planet. This judgment was strictly concerned with *all* men and their evil. This coming judgment had nothing to do with other creatures such as angels. If this judgment had to do with angels in any sense, it seems the Lord would have said or implied He was sorry that He had made the angels. There is absolutely nothing like this in the context of Genesis 6 or the entire Word of God.

"And the LORD was sorry that He had made man on the earth, and He was grieved in His heart.[27] And the LORD said, "I will blot out man whom I have created from the face of the land, from man to animals to creeping things and to birds of the sky; for I am sorry that I have made them" (Gen. 6:6-7). The Word is exceptionally clear that He was sorry He had made man therefore "I will blot out man whom I have created from the face of the land, from man to animals to creeping things and to birds of the sky; for I am sorry that I have made them.' It must be noted here that 'sorry'[28] is from the word וַיִּנָּחֶם (the root נחם)

---

[26] Later Jeremiah said it well: "The heart is more deceitful than all else And is desperately sick; Who can understand it?" (Jer. 17:9) and so did Christ Jesus as the Creator: "For from within, out of the heart of men, proceed the evil thoughts, fornications, thefts, murders, adulteries, 22 deeds of coveting *and* wickedness, *as well as* deceit, sensuality, envy, slander, pride *and* foolishness" (Mark 7:21-22).

[27] וַיִּנָּחֶם יְהֹוָה כִּי־עָשָׂה אֶת־הָאָדָם בָּאָרֶץ וַיִּתְעַצֵּב אֶל־לִבּוֹ׃ The word נחם has the basic meaning to have compassion, to pity, to grieve, to be sorry. (Langenscheidt).

[28] This appears to be also applied to most of the created animal world and the

which means to show compassion. The compassion displayed is that of bringing any judgment on man or simply any judgment.

But it must be noted the Lord did not and does not want to bring on any judgments especially on man. He takes no delight in this even the death of the wicked, and He makes this very clear. "Say to them, 'As I live!' declares the Lord God, 'I take no pleasure in the death of the wicked, but rather that the wicked turn from his way and live. Turn back, turn back from your evil ways! Why then will you die, O house of Israel?" (Ezekiel 33:11).

The Lord wishes none to perish even at the time of the flood yet there was one man Noah, a preacher of righteousness. "For if God did not spare angels when they sinned, but cast them into hell and committed them to pits of darkness, reserved for judgment; [5] and did not spare the ancient world, but preserved Noah, a preacher of righteousness, with seven others, when He brought a flood upon the world of the ungodly" (2 Peter 2:4-5). The Lord will bring judgments on the ungodly and this is what happened at the time of the flood. He brought a flood on the ungodly men of this world and their habitation, not angels in any sense. The flood was a reality for all men to know and understand. It is a great truth of His Word. When God brings destruction or judgments on anyone or any people, He makes this very clear in His Word. Today many deny the literal six day creation, the literal flood, and the literal cause of the flood. It is as if the blame is on angels not on man the true source of the wickedness for the flood.[29]

---

habitation He created for them. The flood did destroy about everything except Noah and his family with the creatures God selected. False teachers teach against the flood: "For when they maintain this, it escapes their notice that by the word of God *the* heavens existed long ago and *the* earth was formed out of water and by water, [6] through which **the world at that time was destroyed, being flooded with water**" (2 Peter 3:5-6).

[29]Perhaps nothing new like 'the devil made me do it' or the blame game and man is very good at this!!!

"Know this first of all, that in the last days mockers will come with *their* mocking, following after their own lusts, ⁴ and saying, "Where is the promise of His coming? For *ever* since the fathers fell asleep, all continues just as it was from the beginning of creation." ⁵ For when they maintain this, it escapes their notice that by the word of God *the* heavens existed long ago and *the* earth was formed out of water and by water, **⁶ through which the world at that time was destroyed, being flooded with water. ⁷ But the present heavens and earth by His word are being reserved for fire, kept for the day of judgment and destruction of ungodly men.** ⁸ But do not let this one *fact* escape your notice, beloved, that with the Lord one day is as a thousand years, and a thousand years as one day. ⁹ The Lord is not slow about His promise, as some count slowness, **but is patient toward you, not wishing for any to perish but for all to come to repentance**" (2 Peter 3:3-9).

Judgments have happened in the past as the flood, the destruction of Sodom and Gomorrah, the exiles of the northern and southern kingdoms of Israel, other nations, etc. But God always gives clear warning to men to repent (change their minds) about Him and His truth. True faith in Him and His Word, always includes repentance, and His Word is very clear about this.

Are the sons of God angelic beings in Gen. 6:1-4?

There is great speculation here as to who the sons of God are. Scripture does not tell us directly, but there is immediate reference that these sons of God are completely human not angelic beings. Angels or angelic beings as a group have not even been named or alluded to in any of the immediate context. Why bring in angels or mention angels or any combination of an angel-man when there is absolutely no previous reference or immediate reference for this in context.

There is so much information commentators read back into this Text (Gen. 6:1-4), but what is the context, context, context, etc.[30] The verses that have 'the sons of God' in the Hebrew Text are:

> 1) "That the **sons of God** saw that the daughters of men were beautiful; and they took wives for themselves, whomever they chose" (Gen. 6:2).
> 2) "The Nephilim were on the earth in those days, and also afterward, when the **sons of God** came in to the daughters of men, and they bore *children* to them. Those were the mighty men who *were* of old, men of renown" (Gen. 6:4).
> 3) "Now there was a day when the **sons of God** came to present themselves before the LORD, and Satan also came among them" (Job 1:6).
> 4) "Again there was a day when the **sons of God** came to present themselves before the LORD, and Satan also came among them to present himself before the LORD" (Job 2:1).
> 5) "When the morning stars sang together, And all the **sons of God** shouted for joy?" (Job 38:7).

Some take the expression 'sons of God' as a technical term. This would be a term always used in the

---

[30]There is absolutely nothing in the immediate context to permit any other interpretation than the sons of God were a Godly line of men. To even allude these are angels, or half man half angel is simply not there in any biblical sense of hermeneutics.

same way in the Text. If so, then the reading/s back into Gen. 6 from Job would be that 'angels' are the 'sons of God.' It is usually acknowledged that Job was referring to angels as 'sons of God.' This would present no problem as far as context permits. But to read back into Genesis the terms which appear identical as a technical term leaves much room for further investigation. "That the sons of God saw that the daughters of men were beautiful; and they took wives for themselves, whomever they chose" (Gen. 6:2).

Issues for sons of God *not* being angelic beings

One would have to read into Genesis 6:1-4 much information to prove biblically that angels are the sons of God in context. Many of the issues which follow are merely observations for those who believe angels to be the sons of God.

1. Angels are nowhere named/mentioned anywhere in context in Gen. 6.
2. Gen. 6 would/could not be properly understood without Job, and probably Jude 1:6-7.
3. Angels would have to create or morph themselves into real human flesh.
4. These newly created or morphed angelic beings would have to be human/angelic with a new nature.
5. These newly created or morphed angelic beings are not human in any sense.
6. These angelic/humans would be a newly created phylum.
7. These angelic/humans have what attributes? More human? More angelic?

8. These angelic/human creatures existed only antediluvian? So Satan cannot do this? Some say he can, but has not as yet.[31]
9. These angelic/humans would not be in Adam and as such not condemned in Adam.
10. These angelic/humans could not produce a seed in Adam for they are not in Adam.
11. The offspring of this union human/angelic with the daughters of men would be what? This would be the second newly created phylum.
12. It seems strange that the daughters of men would not know that their husbands were not human with no genealogy.
13. As the offspring of the angelic/human and daughters of men is not truly human, seems strange Noah would preach righteousness to them for about 120 years.
14. These angelic/humans would have to be hostile and enemies of God, so the expression 'sons of God' has to be used in the sense of enemies of God.
15. The claim is these children produced by this union are somewhat freaks or non human. There is absolutely no support for any of this in context.
16. If these angelic/humans are enemies, this violates Job 1:6 and 2:1, where 'sons of God' are mentioned, but Satan enters separately in among them.
17. It seems strange that these enemies of God (possibly angels) would rejoice at creation. "When the morning stars sang together, and all the **sons of God** shouted for joy?" (Job 38:7).

---

[31] All angels including Satan cannot create life, they are all creatures having one Creator. The creation cannot rise above the Creator.

18. There is absolutely no reference/s to this in the Chumash.[32]
19. Angels cannot create as God creates.
20. If angels can morph or create flesh to live in, then they did something Christ could not or did not do. He added to Himself a human nature with no admixture of attributes.[33]

There is absolutely no biblical support for sons of God being angels in Gen. 6:1-4. There is absolutely nothing to prove the angels cohabited with women. There is everything that militates against this position in context. So who are the sons of God?

The sons of God

So who are the sons of God in Gen. 6:1-4? One has to depend on context, context, and then context. There is also the biblical reference to these being godly creatures, not some ungodly persons or line. All that can be gleaned from the Text is the sons of God and the daughters of men produced children. These were normal children as given in context. To read more into the Text is simply speculation.

All the passages in the Text, both OT and NT, refer to the sons of God as Godly persons or creatures as angels. There is really nothing to violate this unless one reads more into the Text than is permitted.

> "That the **sons of God** saw that the daughters of men were beautiful; and they took wives for themselves, whomever they chose" (Gen. 6:2).

---

[32] The Hebrew term *Chumash* is a Torah in printed form not a Torah scroll. The word comes from the Hebrew word for five, ḥamesh (חמש) referring to the first five Hebrew books or Pentateuch. .

[33] The Son of God did not become flesh in the sense Jehovah changed Himself into 'flesh.' He added to Himself a human nature.

"The Nephilim were on the earth in those days, and also afterward, when the **sons of God** came in to the daughters of men, and they bore *children* to them. Those were the mighty men who *were* of old, men of renown" (Gen. 6:4). "Now there was a day when the **sons of God** came to present themselves before the LORD, and Satan also came among them" (Job 1:6). "Again there was a day when the **sons of God** came to present themselves before the LORD, and Satan also came among them to present himself before the LORD" (Job 2:1). "When the morning stars sang together, And all the **sons of God** shouted for joy?" (Job 38:7). "Blessed are the peacemakers, for they shall be called **sons of God**" (Mat. 5:9). "For neither can they die anymore, for they are like angels, and are **sons of God**, being sons of the resurrection" (Luke 20:36). "For all who are being led by the Spirit of God, these are **sons of God**" (Rom. 8:14). "For the anxious longing of the creation waits eagerly for the revealing of the **sons of God**" (Rom. 8:19). "For you are all **sons of God** through faith in Christ Jesus" (Gal. 3:26).

The reference/s to having normal children is given in the Text. "Now it came about, when **men began to multiply** on the face of the land, and **daughters were born to them**, that **the sons of God saw that the daughters of men were beautiful; and they took**[34] **wives for themselves**, whomever they chose" (Gen. 6:1-2).

---

[34] The וַיִּרְאוּ בְנֵי־הָאֱלֹהִים אֶת־בְּנוֹת הָאָדָם כִּי טֹבֹת הֵנָּה וַיִּקְחוּ לָהֶם נָשִׁים מִכֹּל אֲשֶׁר בָּחָרוּ normal word to take as a wife or wives is לָקַח **take ...** *be taken in marriage;* Francis Brown, Samuel Rolles Driver and Charles Augustus Briggs, *Enhanced Brown-Driver-Briggs Hebrew and English Lexicon*, electronic ed. (Oak Harbor, WA: Logos Research Systems, 2000), 542.

The expression in Hebrew to take as a wife or wives commonly uses the word לָקַח 'to take'[35] (Jud. 3:6; Gen. 12:5; 21:21; 24:3-4; 24:7; 24:37-38; 24:40; many more vss). This would be a normal Hebraic construction to take a wife i.e. a man and woman and nothing else. There is not a hint of anything else angels, angelic beings, angel-human, etc. but a male and a female taken in marriage.

Then the LORD said, "My Spirit shall not strive with man forever, because he also is flesh; nevertheless his days shall be one hundred and twenty years." One possibility of the sin which may be in Gen. 6:2 is that the sons of God were not discerning in any sense as to whom they chose as a wife.[36] This would be in conjunction with the promised seed of Gen. 3:15. There should be a very great discernment on the Godly woman and the preservation of a seed line. This was always a problem from Gen. 3:15. This is very crucial to understand for from Gen 3:15 is the first preaching of the Gospel. "And I will put enmity between you and the woman, and between your seed and her seed; He shall bruise you on the head, and you shall bruise him on the heel" (Gen 3:15).

One may not realize the magnitude of this verse for before the promise/covenant with Abraham, the promise was that of a seed of woman who would destroy the enemy. True faith up to Abraham was taking the side of the seed of the woman, not the side of the serpent. There should have been great reverence and discernment over this great truth. Perhaps in Gen. 6:1-2 there was no growing discernment over the promise in 3:15, possibly no discernment whatever. But there was a man named Noah and his family.

---

[35] Ibid.
[36] The term the sons of God took wives for themselves is the normal use of the language to take in marriage. They took wives but was the discernment there for the Godly line to be preserved from Gen. 3:15?

The nephilim

There is always the additional question who are or is the nephilim? The term 'nephilim' is simply a transliteration from the Hebrew and the expression from Hebrew ending in 'im' is always plural meaning 3 or more. There is nothing mystical about this word or term unless one reads too much into meaning.

As the nephilim are mentioned twice biblically, it seems there are many who read much too much into the meaning. The word does not have to be capitalized as it is only a transliteration of the terminology. Certain truths can be gleaned from the context of these two verses.

1) "The Nephilim were on the earth in those days, and also afterward, when the sons of God came in to the daughters of men, and they bore *children* to them. Those were the mighty men who *were* of old, men of renown" (Gen. 6:4).
2) "There also we saw the Nephilim (the sons of Anak are part of the Nephilim); and we became like grasshoppers in our own sight, and so we were in their sight" (Num. 13:33).

The nephilim were not the product/by product of the sons of God and daughters of men's marriages as they (the nephilim) were already there on the earth. The nephilim seemed to be a rather large group of persons as the "Nephilim (the sons of Anak are part of the Nephilim); and we became like grasshoppers in our own sight, and so we were in their sight" (Num. 13:33) "The **Nephilim** (this word occurs only here and in Gen. 6:4;… were **of great size**; and the Anakites (cf. Num. 13:22), who descended from the Nephilim, were also "strong and tall" (Deut. 9:2).[37]

There is not much more we can glean from this except, this group or name for a people was that of a rather strong and powerful people. There is always the possibility the word or term is being used against any kind of mythology or pagan beliefs being read back into the Text. The writer then is refuting pagan beliefs by declaring His truth concerning the nephilim. There are many writers today who write many things about the nephilim. One should be aware of the source/s. There is only one Source of the Truth and that is His inerrant Word. Anything else is speculation.

Jude 1:5-7

The context of Jude 1:5-7

Jude was encouraging and exhorting believers to contend earnestly for the faith. "Beloved, while I was making every effort to write you about our common salvation, I felt the necessity to write to you appealing that you contend earnestly for the faith which was once for all delivered to the saints" (Jude 1:3).

The believers were to contend earnestly[38] for the faith[39] because an ungodly element had surreptitiously wormed their way in and were changing His saving grace into complete decadence. "For certain persons have crept in unnoticed, those

---

[37] Eugene H. Merrill, "Numbers" In , in *The Bible Knowledge Commentary: An Exposition of the Scriptures*, ed. J. F. Walvoord and R. B. Zuck (Wheaton, IL: Victor Books, 1985), Nu 13:30–33.

[38] [UBS] ἐπαγωνίζομαι struggle in behalf of; [Friberg] ἐπαγωνίζομαι make a strenuous effort on behalf of, struggle for [Liddell Scott] ἐπαγωνίζομαι... *to contend with;*

[39] This would be the complete embodiment of His truth. This included the gospel of faith in Him and His work plus nothing. The false teachers were turning His grace that saves into complete abandonment of Him and His work in them. The false teachers were bringing in all forms of sensuality.

who were long beforehand marked out for this condemnation, ungodly persons who turn the grace of our God into licentiousness and deny our only Master and Lord, Jesus Christ" (Jude 1:4). Jude was warning the believers about the apostates who had slipped into the fold relatively unnoticed.

Jude 1:5-7 is one paragraph

Jude 1:5-7 in the Greek New Testament is one paragraph and in reality one unit of thought. Jude was warning of the current and continuing apostasy which they were facing. He was also presenting God's judgments on ungodly apostates.

There are three completely separate divine judgments on three separate apostate groups (1:5-7) yet they all go together. What they all have in common is they were all judged by God on the basis of their apostasy. Jude was warning the readers to contend for the faith as there was the danger/s of apostasy primarily apostates who have 'crept in unnoticed.'[40] "Jude first warned his readers of the peril of apostasy by citing three examples from the past of apostates who were destroyed (vv. 5–7),[41] and then by describing the upcoming judgment on present apostates (vv. 8–16)."[42] Jude is very clearly presenting three

---

[40][UBS] παρεισδύω sneak in under false pretenses or slip in unnoticed; [Friberg] παρεισδύω or παρεισδύνω 1aor. παρεισέδυσα; 2aor. pass. παρεισεδύησα (JU 4); *slip in (stealthily), join a group unnoticed, worm one's way in*; second aorist passive with the intransitive meaning *sneak in;*
[41]"Now I desire to remind you, though you know all things once for all, that the Lord, after saving a people out of the land of Egypt, **subsequently destroyed those who did not believe**" (Jude 1:5). "And angels who did not keep their own domain, but abandoned their proper abode, **He has kept in eternal bonds under darkness** for the judgment of the great day" (Jude 1:6). "Just as Sodom and Gomorrah and the cities around them, since they in the same way as these indulged in gross immorality and went after strange flesh, are exhibited as an example, **in undergoing the punishment of eternal fire**" (Jude 1:7).
[42] Edward C. Pentecost, "Jude" In , in *The Bible Knowledge Commentary: An Exposition of the Scriptures*, ed. J. F. Walvoord and R. B. Zuck (Wheaton, IL: Victor Books, 1985), Jud 5–16.

distinct apostate groups and their judgments from God.

1. After the exodus from Egypt, the Lord destroyed **those** (*Israelites*) who did not believe (1:5).
2. He has kept **angels** in eternal bonds who abandoned their creature or primary estate (1:6).
3. **Sodom and Gomorrah and the surrounding cities** He has exhibited as an example suffering eternal fire (1:7).

The groups involved and their sins of apostasy are well defined by Jude. Their judgment or destruction is also well defined by Jude. There is no mixing or admixture of the sins or judgments of these three separate groups. The following is a quote from the BKC.[43]

    1.   EGYPT (v. 5)

V. 5. Egypt is mentioned as a reminder of the fact that **most Israelites who left Egypt <u>were not faithful</u>**. An entire generation perished in the wilderness because of their unbelief (cf. Heb. 3:16–19).

    2.   angels (v. 6)

V. 6. Among the **angels** were those who had remained in their first abode and had been obedient to God. But others rebelled and <u>**left their first positions of authority**</u> and are now **in darkness, bound ... for judgment on the Great Day...**

    3.   SODOM AND GOMORRAH (v. 7)

V. 7. Jude's third illustration, of **Sodom and Gomorrah and the surrounding towns**, serves as a dreadful example of what happens to those who <u>**turn from God to follow their own lustful natures**</u>. The fate of the unbelievers in those two cities (Gen. 19:1–29) foreshadows the fate of those who deny God's truth and ignore His warnings. The punishment by fire on the

---

[43] *The Bible Knowledge Commentary: An Exposition of the Scriptures*, ed. J. F. Walvoord and R. B. Zuck (Wheaton, IL: Victor Books, 1985)

perverse inhabitants of Sodom and Gomorrah illustrates the **eternal fire** of hell, which will be experienced by false teachers.[44]

Each apostate group is completely distinct.

Apostate group	Their apostasy or sin	God's judgment
Israelites who came out from Egypt (1:5)	Who did not believe	God destroyed
Angels (1:6)	Who abandoned their creature or created purpose	God placed in eternal bonds until the day of judgment
Sodom and Gomorrah and the cities around them (1:7)	Who chose total sexual perversion	God destroyed as a public display of eternal judgment

It must be noted that Jude has presented three separate apostate groups with three separate apostasies with three separate judgments. All three groups have their listed sin/s i.e. exactly what they did as apostates. All three separate groups have their complete separate sins or apostasies listed and their complete separate God ordained judgments. There is no mixing of any of these details for any of these groups. The fact is God judged these apostates and the great warning of apostasy should be well understood by all believers.

---

[44]Edward C. Pentecost, "Jude" In , in *The Bible Knowledge Commentary: An Exposition of the Scriptures*, ed. J. F. Walvoord and R. B. Zuck (Wheaton, IL: Victor Books, 1985), Jud 5–7.

Does Jude 1:6-7 prove angelic cohabitation?

The support for angelic cohabitation is often provided by reading the sin of Sodom and Gomorrah of perverted cohabitation of Jude 1:7 back into Jude 1:6.

> "And angels who did not keep their own domain, but abandoned their proper abode, He has kept in eternal bonds under darkness for the judgment of the great day" (1:6); "Just as Sodom and Gomorrah and the cities around them, since they in the same way as **these** indulged in gross immorality and went after strange flesh, are exhibited as an example, in undergoing the punishment of eternal fire" (1:7).

The claim is that since 'these' in Greek is a masculine plural it can only refer back to the angels in 1:6. "Just as Sodom and Gomorrah and the cities around them, **since they in the same way as τούτοις these**[45] **(these referring to angels in verse 6)** indulged in gross immorality and went after strange flesh, are exhibited as an example, in undergoing the punishment of eternal fire (Jude 1:6-7). All this stems from the use of **τούτοις** in verse 7. These=**τούτοις** is a masculine dative plural and the result would be previous reference back to the angels (masculine accusative plural) in verse 6. So if one holds to angels having sexual relations, the belief is these verses prove this. But do they?

As is well known from Genesis, the sin/s of Sodom and Gomorrah, there is the inclusion of several cities around them (Sodom and Gomorrah) doing the same sexual perversion/s. It

---

[45] ὡς Σόδομα καὶ Γόμορρα καὶ αἱ περὶ αὐτὰς πόλεις τὸν ὅμοιον τρόπον **τούτοις** ἐκπορνεύσασαι καὶ ἀπελθοῦσαι ὀπίσω σαρκὸς ἑτέρας, πρόκεινται δεῖγμα πυρὸς αἰωνίου δίκην ὑπέχουσαι (Jude 1:7). The nearest reference would be angels. Yet there may be another option which will be presented later.

must be noted the feminine participles[46] referring to all the cities i.e. Sodom and Gomorrah and the cities around them. "Just as Sodom and Gomorrah and the cities **around them**, since they in the same way as these **indulged** in gross immorality and **went after** strange flesh, are exhibited as an example, **in undergoing** the punishment of eternal fire."

- Just as Sodom and Gomorrah and **the cities (feminine plural)** around **them (feminine plural)**
- since they in the same way as <u>**these**</u> **(masculine dative plural)**
- **indulged** ἐκπορνεύσασαι **(feminine plural)** in gross immorality and
- **went after** ἀπελθοῦσαι **(feminine plural)** strange flesh, are exhibited πρόκεινται (present passive indicative 3rd person plural) as an example
- **in undergoing** ὑπέχουσαι **(feminine plural)** the punishment of eternal fire.

The key in this is 'these' **τούτοις** (dative masculine plural) in 1:7. The nearest antecedent as understood by many is exclusively the angels in 1:6. So they simply read 1:7 back into 1:6 not only reinterpreting 1:6 but also 1:7. None of this is contextually or grammatically possible. The translation 'in the same way as these or in a similar manner' does not say in exactly the same way i.e. equivalent or equal to. Actually it can't be for if it were exactly the same, it would have to be same sex among the angels as was the primary sin of Sodom and Gomorrah. There would have to be redefinition of the

---

[46] ὡς Σόδομα καὶ Γόμορρα καὶ αἱ περὶ αὐτὰς **(feminine plural)** πόλεις **(feminine plural)** τὸν ὅμοιον τρόπον τούτοις **(masculine dative plural)** ἐκπορνεύσασαι **(feminine plural)** καὶ ἀπελθοῦσαι **(feminine plural)** ὀπίσω σαρκὸς ἑτέρας, πρόκεινται (present passive indicative 3rd person plural) δεῖγμα πυρὸς αἰωνίου δίκην ὑπέχουσαι **(feminine plural)**

sexual practice from verse 1:7 back into 1:6.⁴⁷ One would have to change meanings in context and the sexual sins of Sodom and Gomorrah and the surrounding cities.⁴⁸

Also the participles in 1:7 (all feminine plural)⁴⁹ referring to Sodom and Gomorrah (S&G) and the surrounding cities can't *all* be applied equally to the angels in 1:6. Actually none of the participles apply to the angels in any sense as can be seen in the following paradigm.

Participles⁵⁰ 1:7	Translation	Comments
ἐκπορνεύσασαι (aorist active feminine plural)	live immorally, indulge in excessive blatant depravity, be given to fornication	S&G and surrounding cities were fully given over to depraved sex. This cannot be said of angels.

---

[47] "And angels who did not keep their own domain, but abandoned their proper abode (Jude 1:6) **[Just as Sodom and Gomorrah and the cities around them, since they In the same way as <u>these</u> (angels in vs. 6) indulged in gross immorality and went after strange flesh, are exhibited as an example, in undergoing the punishment of eternal fire"(Jude 1:7)]** He has kept in eternal bonds under darkness for the judgment of the great day." (Jude 1:6-7). One cannot just read one verse back into another and redefine the meaning in context especially of both verses. Jude was just using these apostates as examples not teaching angelic sex practices or cohabitation. Those who hold to this have missed the entire contextual meaning of these verses.

[48] There is no proof for any same sex angelic sins as some want to prove angelic cohabitation. One cannot read into the Text something that is not there.

[49] ὡς Σόδομα καὶ Γόμορρα καὶ αἱ περὶ αὐτὰς **(feminine plural)** πόλεις **(feminine plural)** τὸν ὅμοιον τρόπον **τούτοις (masculine dative plural)** ἐκπορνεύσασαι **(feminine plural)** καὶ ἀπελθοῦσαι **(feminine plural)** ὀπίσω σαρκὸς ἑτέρας, πρόκεινται (present passive indicative 3ʳᵈ person plural) δεῖγμα πυρὸς αἰωνίου δίκην ὑπέχουσαι **(feminine plural)**

[50] All these participles have equal application to Sodom and Gomorrah (S&G) and surrounding cities (1:7)

ἀπελθοῦσαι (aorist active feminine plural) ὀπίσω σαρκὸς ἑτέρας,	Indulge in unnatural sex acts;	S&G and surrounding cities sexually went after other 'flesh' which was perverse. This can't be said of angels.
πρόκεινται δεῖγμα πυρὸς αἰωνίου δίκην **ὑπέχουσαι** (present active feminine plural)	continually exhibited or viewed as an example, in undergoing the punishment of eternal fire.	S&G and surrounding cities judged as examples and can be literally viewed near the Dead Sea. This can't be said of angels in bonds of darkness who can't be viewed.

The judgment of Sodom and Gomorrah and the cities around them is not identical to that of these angels: "Sodom and Gomorrah and the surroundings cities He has exhibited[51] as an example suffering eternal fire" (1:7). This is an ongoing example which the readers would be well versed and knew from history. The final judgment is totally different for the angels as 'He has kept them in eternal bonds under darkness for the judgment of the great day" (1:6). The other participles cannot be applied either.

---

[51] πρόκεινται (present passive indicative 3rd person plural) δεῖγμα πυρὸς αἰωνίου δίκην

There is a simple answer

Yet there is a solution which might be best for those who are looking for a biblical explanation to this seemingly complex issue. "And angels who did not keep their own domain, but abandoned their proper abode, He has kept in eternal bonds under darkness for the judgment of the great day" (Jud 1:6). As this group of angels did not keep their primary estate, they abandoned their proper domain for which God had created them. They abandoned their doxological domain primarily giving help to His heirs: "Are they not all ministering spirits, sent out to render service for the sake of those who will inherit salvation?" (Heb 1:14). Lenski makes this observation: "Instead of keeping the high, glorious ἀρχή, rule and domain, assigned them by God (ἑαυτῶν, possessive genitive: "belonging to themselves") they were dissatisfied, wanted a still higher domain that did not belong to them, and left their own οἰκητήριον, "habitation" – we may say the capital from which they were by God designed to rule – as not being grand enough for them."[52] "And angels (**τε**)[53] who did not keep their own domain." Note the position of the particle **τε** in 1:6 after angels ἀγγέλους "ἀγγέλους **τε** τοὺς μὴ τηρήσαντας τὴν ἑαυτῶν ἀρχὴν" (1:6). The grammatical use of **τε** in this verse is essential to understand for the proper interpretation. Verse 1:5 prior to 1:6 is connected by the connective particle **τε**.

"Now I desire to remind you, though you know all things once for all, that the Lord, after saving a people out of the land of Egypt, subsequently destroyed **those who did not**

---

[52]R. C. H. Lenski, *The Interpretation of The Epistles of St. Peter, St. John, and St. Jude*, (Minneapolis, Minn: Augsburg Publishing House, 1966), 619.
[53]The connective particle **τε** after 'angels' in verse 1:6. "**τέ** ... enclitic particle ... **marker of close relationship between sequential states or events, *and likewise, and so, so* ... Jude 6.**" William Arndt, Frederick W. Danker, and Walter Bauer, *A Greek-English Lexicon of the New Testament and Other Early Christian Literature* (Chicago: University of Chicago Press, 2000), 993.

believe and angels (τε) who did not keep their own domain, but abandoned their proper abode, He has kept in eternal bonds under darkness for the judgment of the great day" (1:5-6)

"Ὑπομνῆσαι δὲ ὑμᾶς βούλομαι, εἰδότας [ὑμᾶς] πάντα ὅτι [ὁ] κύριος ἅπαξ λαὸν ἐκ γῆς Αἰγύπτου σώσας τὸ δεύτερον **τοὺς μὴ πιστεύσαντας** ἀπώλεσεν **ἀγγέλους τε**[54] τοὺς μὴ τηρήσαντας τὴν ἑαυτῶν ἀρχὴν ἀλλὰ ἀπολιπόντας τὸ ἴδιον οἰκητήριον εἰς κρίσιν μεγάλης ἡμέρας δεσμοῖς ἀϊδίοις ὑπὸ ζόφον τετήρηκεν" (1:5-6).[55]

The connective particle τε is making a definitive connection from 'the angels' in verse (1:6 to) 'those who did not believe' (1:5). The writer is simply connecting these two groups together as examples. 'Those who did not believe and angels' (1:5-6) are considered closely connected or better inseparable by means of the grammatical use of the particle τε.

So the following verse (1:7) is referring to or referencing verses (1:5-6) together not just verse 1:6. "Just as Sodom and Gomorrah and the cities around them, since they in the same way as these (*those who did not believe and angels 1:5-6*) indulged in gross immorality and went after strange flesh, are exhibited as an example, in undergoing the punishment of

---

[54] The connective particle **τε** is joining the angelic sin and apostasy (1:6) to the apostasy of Israelites who did not believe (1:5).

[55] "Now I desire to remind you, though you know all things once for all, that the Lord, after saving a people out of the land of Egypt, subsequently destroyed **those who did not believe**" (Jude 1:5). "**And angels** who did not keep their own domain, but abandoned their proper abode, He has kept in eternal bonds under darkness for the judgment of the great day" (Jude 1:6). "**those who did not believe**" (Jude 1:5) is directly connected to "**And angels**" by the particle τε. Those who did not believe and angels are *directly* connected as one group. So the reference from 1:7 should look like this: "Just as Sodom and Gomorrah and the cities around them, since they in the same way as **these** (**those who did not believe and angels 1:5-6**) indulged in gross immorality and went after strange flesh, are exhibited as an example, in undergoing the punishment of eternal fire" (Jude 1:7). "These" of 1:7 simply is connected to both previous groups not just one.

eternal fire" (Jude1:7). ὡς⁵⁶ Σόδομα καὶ Γόμορρα καὶ αἱ περὶ αὐτὰς πόλεις τὸν ὅμοιον τρόπον **τούτοις** ἐκπορνεύσασαι καὶ ἀπελθοῦσαι ὀπίσω σαρκὸς ἑτέρας, πρόκεινται δεῖγμα πυρὸς αἰωνίου δίκην ὑπέχουσαι (1:7)⁵⁷

"The anarthrous and qualitative "angels' lets us feel how great they were, how high they stood. τε = "too" and connects more closely than καὶ would. Israel and the angels belong together in a way that cannot include Sodom, etc. The apposition: "those that did not keep," etc. specifies which class of angels is referred to."⁵⁸ The **τε** is drawing the apostates in 1:6 to those in 1:7 as two apostate groups together. The τούτοις is in verse 1:7 is referring back to the Israelites in 1:5 and to the angels in 1:6.

1) Israelites who did not believe (1:5)
2) Angels who did not keep their own domain (1:6)

"Verse 6 is closely connected to v.5 by τε although the sin of the angels is very different from the sin of the unbelieving Israelites. In Jude's estimation the point to be noted is not similarity of sin but irrevocable and terrible judgment. So Jude connects v. 7 with v. 5 (not with v. 6 alone). This connection does not lie in ὡς; it lies in τὸν ὅμοιον τρόπον τούτοις, the adverbial accusative; "in similar manner to these" and "these" is masculine and refers to "angels that kept not," etc., (v.6) and to "those that did not believe" (Israelites, verse 5). The reference must be to both because τε connect them so closely. With this adverbial accusative Jude says that this third case is *similar* to

---

[56] The comparison ὡς is comparing the apostasy of Sodom and Gomorrah and the cities around them to the two preceding apostate groups of angels and the unbelieving Israelites.
[57] Just as Sodom and Gomorrah and the cities around them, since they in the same way as these indulged in gross immorality and went after strange flesh, are exhibited as an example, in undergoing the punishment of eternal fire. (Jude1:7)
[58] R. C. H. Lenski, *The Interpretation of The Epistles of St. Peter, St. John, and St. Jude*, (Minneapolis, Minn: Augsburg Publishing House, 1966), 618.

both the other cases. The translation "like" for ὅμοιον is inexact (our versions). The similarity does not lie in the sins, for that of the Israelites is unbelief, that of the angels is not unbelief nor is that of Sodom, etc. The similarity lies in the fact that all these *sinners*, unbelieving Israelites, rebel angels, fornicating Sodomites, *received a final, eternal penalty*."[59]

As Jude simply developed three distinct judgments of apostates, it would be quite normal to read Jude 1:6 as complete[60] into 1:7. Reading 1:6 of angels leaving their first abode does not change meaning in verse 1:7. The reverse of reading most or all of 1:7 into 1:6 redefines verse 6. This makes no sense at all and does not really equate to anything but confusion with the immediate Text.

Conclusion

There is absolutely no proof that angels cohabited with women in Gen. 6:1-4. His inerrant Word is very clear and gives much support for what is happening in Genesis especially Genesis 6:1-4. No one needs Job, Jude, Isaiah or any other Text to read back into these verses for interpretation, better re-interpretation. Again, what is the context? Is this part of the context?

The saying used to be always context, context, and context. Jude cannot be used to prove any sort of angelic cohabitation. Jude never wrote his epistle for anything but contending earnestly for the faith (Jude 1:3). Jude simply presented three types of apostate judgments as warnings to the readers. If he did allude to some pagan mythology or even reference it (which might be debated), he may have done this to refute it, not read it back into the Text as some supportive truth.

---

[59]Ibid., 622-23.
[60]Jude 1:5-7…'complete' as the sin/s described for each apostate group and each group's specific judgment.

The last Adam and His cross, His priesthood, His kingdom

"So also it is written, the first man, Adam, became a living soul. The last Adam *became* a life-giving spirit. However, the spiritual is not first, but the natural; then the spiritual. The first man is from the earth, earthy; the second man is from heaven"
(1 Cor. 15:45-47).[1]

The first and last Adam

With these very commanding verses (1 Cor. 15:45-47), Paul compares the work of the first man Adam to that of the last Adam who is Christ. "The term *last Adam* is found only once in the Bible (1 Cor. 15:45) and is generally considered synonymous to the expression *second man*, found also in this passage in 1 Corinthians 15:47. The idea involved in this terminology is that Christ is head of the new creation composed of all those who are in Christ as compared to Adam, head of the old creation, composed of all those who are in Adam."[2] All men are born in Adam as he is head of the entire human race. And all will die in Adam, "for as in Adam all die, so also in Christ all shall be made alive" (1 Cor. 15:22).[3] "**Death came** to all those related to Adam by natural birth because of the disobedience of one **man**. As the father of mankind Adam in his sin brought death to everybody (cf. Gen. 3:17–19; Rom. 5:12).

---

[1] οὕτως καὶ γέγραπται· ἐγένετο ὁ **πρῶτος ἄνθρωπος Ἀδὰμ** εἰς ψυχὴν ζῶσαν, **ὁ ἔσχατος Ἀδὰμ** εἰς πνεῦμα ζῳοποιοῦν. ⁴⁶ ἀλλ' οὐ πρῶτον τὸ πνευματικὸν ἀλλὰ τὸ ψυχικόν, ἔπειτα τὸ πνευματικόν. ⁴⁷ ὁ **πρῶτος ἄνθρωπος** ἐκ γῆς χοϊκός, ὁ **δεύτερος ἄνθρωπος** ἐξ οὐρανοῦ.
[2] John F. Walvoord, "The Present Work of Christ in Heaven," *Bibliotheca Sacra* 121 (1964): 196.
[3] ὥσπερ γὰρ ἐν τῷ Ἀδὰμ πάντες ἀποθνήσκουσιν, οὕτως καὶ ἐν τῷ Χριστῷ πάντες **ζῳοποιηθήσονται** (1 Cor. 15:22).

But because of the obedience (Phil. 2:8) of another **Man** (1 Tim. 2:5) **resurrection** will come to **all** those related to Him by spiritual birth. Paul would later expand this grand truth in his letter to the Romans (Rom. 5:12–19)."[4]

Paul presented the totally contrasting work of Adam and the work of Christ very clearly in Romans 5:12-21. It is essential to understand man's condemned state in Adam and eternal life in Christ Jesus.

> "Therefore, just as through one man sin entered into the world **(work of Adam)**, and death through sin **(work of Adam)**, and so death spread to all men, because all sinned-- [13] for until the Law sin was in the world **(work of Adam)**; but sin is not imputed when there is no law. [14] Nevertheless death reigned from Adam until Moses **(work of Adam)**, even over those who had not sinned in the likeness of the offense of Adam, who is a type of Him who was to come. [15] But the free gift **(work of Christ)** is not like the transgression **(work of Adam)**. For if by the transgression of the one the many died **(work of Adam)**, much more did the grace of God and the gift by the grace of the one Man, Jesus Christ, abound to the many **(work of Christ)**. [16] And the gift **(work of Christ)** is not like *that which came* through the one who sinned **(work of Adam)**; for on the one hand the judgment *arose* from one *transgression* resulting in condemnation **(work of Adam)**, but on the other hand the free gift **(work of Christ)** *arose* from many transgressions resulting in justification **(work of Christ)**. [17] For if by the transgression of the one **(work of Adam)**, death reigned through the one **(work of Adam)**, much

---

[4] David K. Lowery, "1 Corinthians," in *The Bible Knowledge Commentary: An Exposition of the Scriptures*, ed. J. F. Walvoord and R. B. Zuck, vol. 2 (Wheaton, IL: Victor Books, 1985), 543.

more those who receive the abundance of grace and of the gift of righteousness *(**work of Christ**)* will reign in life through the One, Jesus Christ. [18] So then as through one transgression there resulted condemnation to all men *(**work of Adam**)*, even so through one act of righteousness there resulted justification of life to all men *(**work of Christ**)*. [19] For as through the one man's disobedience the many were made sinners *(**work of Adam**)*, even so through the obedience of the One the many will be made righteous *(**work of Christ**)*. [20] And the Law came in that the transgression might increase; but where sin increased, grace abounded all the more, [21] that, as sin reigned in death, even so grace might reign through righteousness to eternal life through Jesus Christ our Lord *(**work of Christ**)*" (Rom. 5:12-21).

Sin came into the world through the one man Adam. All men are condemned in Adam. Man is a condemned sinner at conception[5] in need of God's provided righteousness to deliver him from eternal condemnation (Rom. 1:16-17).

The work of Adam (Rom. 5:12-21)
1. Therefore, just as through one man sin entered into the world *(**work of Adam**)*,
2. and death through sin *(**work of Adam**)*,
3. Nevertheless death reigned from Adam until Moses *(**work of Adam**)*,

---

[5] "Behold, I was brought forth in iniquity, And in sin my mother conceived me" (Ps. 51:5). "David then acknowledged that he was morally impotent. He was born **a sinner**, that is, at no time in his life was he without sin. This ran contrary to God's moral demands on his life. From his early days he faced **inner** tension, knowing that God desires **truth** and **wisdom**, that is, reliable and productive living." Allen P. Ross, "Psalms," in *The Bible Knowledge Commentary: An Exposition of the Scriptures*, ed. J. F. Walvoord and R. B. Zuck, vol. 1 (Wheaton, IL: Victor Books, 1985), 832.

4. over those who had not sinned in the likeness of the offense of Adam *(work of Adam)*,
5. not like the transgression *(work of Adam)*.
6. For if by the transgression of the one the many died *(work of Adam)*
7. through the one who sinned *(work of Adam)*;
8. judgment *arose* from one *transgression* resulting in condemnation *(work of Adam)*,
9. For if by the transgression of the one *(work of Adam)*,
10. death reigned through the one *(work of Adam)*
11. So then as through one transgression *(work of Adam)*
12. there resulted condemnation to all men *(work of Adam)*
13. For as through the one man's disobedience *(work of Adam)*
14. the many were made sinners *(work of Adam)*,
15. that, as sin reigned in death *(work of Adam)*

The work of Christ (Rom. 5:12-21)

1. But the free gift *(work of Christ)*
2. much more did the grace of God *(work of Christ)*
3. the gift by the grace of the one Man, Jesus Christ, abound to the many *(work of Christ)*
4. And the gift *(work of Christ)*
5. but on the other hand the free gift *(work of Christ)*
6. resulting in justification *(work of Christ)*
7. much more those who receive the abundance of grace *(work of Christ)*
8. the gift of righteousness will reign in life through the One, Jesus Christ *(work of Christ)*
9. through one act of righteousness *(work of Christ)*
10. there resulted justification of life to all men *(work of Christ)*
11. even so through the obedience of the One *(work of Christ)*
12. the many will be made righteous *(work of Christ)*
13. grace abounded all the more *(work of Christ)*
14. even so grace might reign *(work of Christ)*
15. through righteousness to eternal life through Jesus Christ our Lord *(work of Christ)*

All men are condemned in Adam

It must be continually kept in focus that Paul was comparing the first Adam to Christ. This concerns primarily Adam's sin and Christ's great passion that is His cross for the sins of the world (John 1:29; 3:16; 16:8; 1 John 2:2). Man cannot conceive how the Creator of this present universe could or would come down from His glory only to become the greatest Servant ever and die for our sin (Mat. 20:28; Mark 10:45).

This proves why one must understand the greatness of the last Adam and His person and His work. There are several very critical issues which must be addressed from Rom. 5:12-21. Sin came into the world through one man, i.e. Adam and not angels. As sin began in the angelic realm with Satan in heaven, sin and death did not come into this world but by one man. There was no sin or death in the world before Adam. This is made very clear by the Text (Rom. 5:12).

It is also made very clear that death came to all men in that all sinned in Adam. "Therefore, just as through one man sin entered into the world, and death through sin, and so **death spread to all men, because all sinned**" (Rom. 5:12). When did all men sin? They all sinned in Adam. Adam did not represent the human race for the whole race was in Adam when Adam first sinned. That one sin made condemned sinners of the entire human race. This does not mean the human race pre-existed, but the whole race is seen by God as sinning in Adam when Adam sinned. This can also be supported by Heb. 7:9-10.[6]

---

[6] God sees Levi paying tithes through Abraham, and it is essential to see how God sees things theistically not as man sees them. "And, so to speak, through Abraham even Levi, who received tithes, paid tithes, [10] for he was still in the loins of his father when Melchizedek met him" (Heb 7:9-10). The personal superiority of Melchizedek over the patriarch Abraham is guaranteed by the fact that **Abraham gave him a 10th of the plunder**. And though Melchizedek had no connections with the Levitical order, still he both received this tithe from **Abraham and blessed him**. This act of blessing reinforced his superiority to the patriarch. Moreover, he was evidently superior to the Levites as well, who collected tithes but were nonetheless subject to death. By contrast the tithe collected from Abraham was collected **by him who is declared to be living**. Furthermore, in a sense Levi paid the tithe **through Abraham because ... Levi was still in the body of his ancestor**. The original expression, rendered **one might even say**, probably means something like "so to speak." The writer knew that Levi did not literally pay tithes to Melchizedek, but on the principle that an ancestor is greater than his descendants, Abraham's act affirmed Melchizedek's superiority even to the Levitical priests themselves. Melchizedek thus has a greatness which the Old Testament record clearly

"Paul had now finished his description of how God has revealed and applied to humans His provided righteousness on the basis of the sacrificial death of Jesus Christ received by faith. One thing remains to be done—to present the contrastive parallelism between the work of Jesus Christ (and its results in justification and reconciliation) and the work of another man, Adam (and its results in sin and death). Paul began by saying, **Therefore** (lit., "because of this"; cf. 4:16), and started his comparison, **just as;** but he became concerned by other matters and did not return to the comparison until 5:15. Paul explained that **sin** (in Gr., "the sin") **entered** (*eisēlthen*, "entered into") **the world through one man; and,** in accord with God's warning (cf. Gen. 2:16–17), **death** (in Gr., "the death") **through sin.** God's penalty for sin was both spiritual and physical death (cf. Rom. 6:23; 7:13), and Adam and Eve and their descendants experienced both. But physical death, being an outward, visible experience, is in view in 5:12–21. Paul concluded, **And in this way death** ("the death") **came to all men.** "Came" is *diēlthen*, literally "passed or went through" or "spread through." *Eisēlthen*, "entered into" (the first clause in the verse) means that sin went in the world's front door (by means of Adam's sin); and *diēlthen*, "went through," means that death penetrated the entire human race, like a vapor permeating all of a house's rooms. The reason death spread to all, Paul explained, is that **all sinned.** The Greek past (aorist) tense occurs in all three verbs in this verse. So the entire human race is viewed as having sinned in the one act of Adam's sin (cf. "all have sinned," also the Gr. past tense, in 3:23). Two ways of explaining this participation of the human race in the sin of Adam have been presented by theologians—the "federal headship" of Adam over the race and the "natural or seminal headship" of Adam. (Others say that people merely imitated Adam, that he gave the human race a bad example. But that does not do justice to 5:12.) The federal headship view considers Adam, the first man, as the *representative* of the human race that generated from him. As the representative of all humans, Adam's act of sin was considered by God to be the act of all people and his penalty of death was judicially made the penalty of everybody. The natural headship view, on the other hand, recognizes that the entire human race was seminally and *physically* in Adam, the first man. As a result God considered all people as participating in the act of sin which Adam

---

attests." Zane C. Hodges, "Hebrews," in *The Bible Knowledge Commentary: An Exposition of the Scriptures*, ed. J. F. Walvoord and R. B. Zuck, vol. 2 (Wheaton, IL: Victor Books, 1985), 798.

committed and as receiving the penalty he received. Even adherents of the federal headship view must admit that Adam is the natural head of the human race physically; the issue is the relationship spiritually. Biblical evidence supports the natural headship of Adam. When presenting the superiority of Melchizedek's priesthood to Aaron's, the author of Hebrews argued that Levi, the head of the priestly tribe, "who collects the 10th, paid the 10th through Abraham, because when Melchizedek met Abraham, Levi was still in the body of his ancestor" (Heb. 7:9–10).[7]

Those who hold to a representative view of Adam (federal headship) fail to see the great problems they present with the Text. All men sinned in Adam and are treated as sinners not because Adam represented them. This can be found nowhere in the Text. All men are treated as sinners not for someone's sin, someone else's sin i.e. Adam's sin, they are treated as sinners for all sinned in Adam. All men are eternally condemned for all men sinned in Adam. Adam represented no one but Adam not even Eve. The entire human race was in Adam, and the Scriptures nowhere teach a representative or federal headship of the first man Adam.

> "The Federal theory, or theory of the Covenants, had its origin with Cocceius (1603–1669), professor at Leyden, but was more fully elaborated by Turretin (1623–1687). It has become a tenet of the Reformed as distinguished from the Lutheran church, and in this country it has its main advocates in the Princeton school of theologians, of whom Dr. Charles Hodge was the representative. According to this view, Adam was constituted by God's sovereign appointment the representative of the whole human race. With Adam as their representative, God entered into covenant, agreeing to bestow upon them eternal life on condition of his obedience, but making the penalty of his disobedience to be the corruption and death of all his posterity. In accordance with the terms of this covenant, since Adam sinned, God accounts all his descendants as sinners, and condemns them because of Adam's transgression. In execution of this sentence of condemnation, God immediately creates each soul of Adam's

---

[7] John A. Witmer, "Romans," in *The Bible Knowledge Commentary: An Exposition of the Scriptures*, ed. J. F. Walvoord and R. B. Zuck, vol. 2 (Wheaton, IL: Victor Books, 1985), 458.

posterity with a corrupt and depraved nature, which infallibly leads to sin, and which is itself sin. The theory is therefore a theory of the immediate imputation of Adam's sin to his posterity, their corruption of nature not being the cause of that imputation, but the effect of it. In Rom. 5:12, "death passed unto all men, for that all sinned," signifies: "physical, spiritual, and eternal death came to all, because all were regarded and treated as sinners." ... Federal theory we object: A. It is extra-Scriptural, there being no mention of such a covenant with Adam in the account of man's trial. The assumed allusion to Adam's apostasy in Hosea 6:7, where the word "covenant" is used, is too precarious and too obviously metaphorical to afford the basis for a scheme of imputation (see Henderson, Com. on Minor Prophets, *in loco*). In Heb. 8:8—"new covenant"—there is suggested a contrast, not with an Adamic, but with the Mosaic, covenant (*cf.* verse 9). In Hosea 6:7—"they like Adam [marg. 'men'] have trangressed the covenant" (Rev. Ver.)—the correct translation is given by Henderson, Minor Prophets: "But they, like men that break a covenant, there they proved false to me." LXX; αὐτοὶ δέ εἰσιν ὡς ἄνθρωπος παραβαίνων διαθήκην. De Wette: "Aber sie übertreten den Bund nach Menschenart; daselbst sind sie mir treulos." Here the word *adam*, translated "man," either means "a man," or "man," *i. e.*, generic man. "Israel had as little regard to their covenants with God as men of unprincipled character have for ordinary contracts." "Like a man" = as men do. compare Ps. 82:7—"ye shall die like men"; Hosea 8:1, 2—"they have transgressed my covenant"—an allusion to the Abrahamic or Mosaic covenant. Heb. 8:9—"Behold, the days come, saith the Lord, that I will make a new covenant with the house of Israel and with the house of Judah; Not according to the covenant that I made with their fathers In the day that I took them by the hand to lead them forth out of the land of Egypt." B. It contradicts Scripture, in making the first result of Adam's sin to be God's *regarding and treating* the race as sinners. The Scripture, on the contrary, declares that Adam's offense *constituted* us sinners (Rom. 5:19). We are not sinners simply because God regards and treats us as such, but God regards us as sinners because we are sinners. Death is said to have "passed unto all men," not because all were regarded and treated as sinners, but "because all sinned" (Rom. 5:12).[8]

All men are condemned in Adam and the Scriptures are perfectly clear with this truth. All men were seen by God as

---

[8] Strong, A. H. (1907). *Systematic theology* (612–616). Philadelphia: American Baptist Publication Society.

having sinned in Adam and their eternal condemnation is based on all sinning in the one man Adam in that one sin (Gen. 3:1-22). All men are in Adam and all will die in Adam unless they turn to the last Adam. "For as in Adam all die, so also in Christ all shall be made alive" (1 Cor. 15:22); "So also it is written, the first man, Adam, became a living soul. The last Adam *became* a life-giving spirit" (1 Cor. 15:45). The same 'soul' or immaterial part in Adam is what is passed on to all men for 'all men are in Adam." They become living souls in Adam at conception, but that immaterial part or soul from Adam is dead with God.

All men are in Adam and condemned with the full nature of Adam. God does not create a new soul known as 'creationism' which becomes a sinful soul[9] by placing it in man at conception. All men have Adam's nature for they are all in Adam. Christ Jesus was never in Adam. He was never a condemned sinner but He was treated as one on the Cross (Is. 53:10; 2 Cor. 5:21).

- "Therefore, just as through one man sin entered into the world, and death through sin, and so death spread to all men, because all sinned" (Rom. 5:12).
- "For if by the transgression of the one the many died" (5:15).

---

[9] "Creationism. This view is to the effect that each individual soul is to be regarded as an immediate creation of God, owing its origin to a direct creative act, of which the time cannot be precisely determined. The soul is supposed to be created pure, but united with a depraved body. This need not necessarily mean that the soul is created first *in separation from the body*, and then polluted by being brought in contact with the body, which would seem to assume that sin is something physical. It may simply mean that the soul, though called into being by a creative act of God, yet is pre-formed in the physical life of the fetus, that is, in the life of the parents, and thus acquires its life not above and outside of, but under and in, that complex of sin by which humanity as a whole is burdened." L. Berkhof, *Systematic Theology* (Grand Rapids, MI., WM. B. Erdmans Publishing Co., 1941), 199.

- "The judgment *arose* from one *transgression* resulting in condemnation" (5:16).
- "For if by the transgression of the one, death reigned through the one" (5:17).
- "So then as through **one transgression there resulted condemnation to all men**" (5:18).

    It must be clearly understood that man is condemned prior to any personal sins. Personal sins do not condemn a man for he is already condemned in Adam and that at conception. It is often heard that one must give up their sins, repent of their sins, or confess their sins in order to be saved. But, again personal sins were not the reason for condemnation. One must realize he is a condemned sinner in the sight of God and agrees with God that he is a condemned sinner. This is what is meant by confession that is agreeing with God or saying the same things God is saying. God has made this very clear in His Word.
    By not placing faith in Christ, that is His Person and His work *alone* for salvation, one will die in their trespasses and sins. Their trespasses and sins will then add to their eternally condemned state (Eph. 2:1). One must believe Jesus is the Eternal Son of God the God-man Who died for their sins and was raised on the 3rd day. It is all about Him. Again, God cannot die but Jesus is the God-man Who died in the flesh.

God's provision of righteousness for all men

    "So then as through one transgression there resulted condemnation to all men, even so through one act of righteousness there resulted justification of life to all men" (Rom 5:18).10 God provided righteousness (a declaration of being right with Him) for all men that are in His Son Christ Jesus. This is a declaration of being just or right with God based on Christ's provided righteousness from His cross.

This Christ provided righteousness is what condemned man needs and can only be received by grace through faith. Positionally, all men are in Adam, but when they trust Christ for eternal life, they are then in Christ (1 Cor. 15:22).

Paul makes all this perfectly clear in the book of Romans "For I am not ashamed of the gospel, for it is the power of God for salvation to everyone who believes, to the Jew first and also to the Greek. For in it *the* righteousness of God is revealed from faith to faith; as it is written, but the righteous *man* shall live by faith" (Rom 1:16-17). It must be noted there is no article (the) before righteousness in this verse. Might be better to read "for in it *a* righteousness of God is revealed." This righteousness is not one of God's attributes for He does

---

[10] Righteousness and justify, justification are both from the same root word. Ἄρα οὖν ὡς δι' ἑνὸς παραπτώματος εἰς πάντας ἀνθρώπους εἰς κατάκριμα, οὕτως καὶ δι' ἑνὸς **δικαιώματος** εἰς πάντας ἀνθρώπους εἰς **δικαίωσιν** ζωῆς·(Rom 5:18) **δικαιώματος** from δικαίωμα, ατος, τό …a regulation relating to just or right action, *regulation, requirement, commandment* … an action that meets expectations as to what is right or just, *righteous deed* …δι' ἑνὸς δικαιώματος (opposite παράπτωμα) Ro 5:18. William Arndt, Frederick W. Danker, and Walter Bauer, <u>A Greek-English Lexicon of the New Testament and Other Early Christian Literature</u> (Chicago: University of Chicago Press, 2000), 249. **δικαίωσιν** from δικαίωσις, εως, ἡ *justification, vindication, acquittal … acquittal that brings life* 5:18. William Arndt, Frederick W. Danker, and Walter Bauer, <u>A Greek-English Lexicon of the New Testament and Other Early Christian Literature</u> (Chicago: University of Chicago Press, 2000), 250. Note that both words are from the root verb **δικαιόω**… to take up a legal cause, *show justice, do justice, take up a cause* … to render a favorable verdict, *vindicate* as activity of humans *justify, vindicate,* <u>treat as just … be acquitted, be pronounced and treated as righteous</u> and thereby become δίκαιος, receive the divine gift of δικαιοσύνη through faith in Christ Jesus and apart from νόμος as a basis for evaluation, William Arndt, Frederick W. Danker, and Walter Bauer, <u>A Greek-English Lexicon of the New Testament and Other Early Christian Literature</u> (Chicago: University of Chicago Press, 2000), 249.

not share those with anyone. This is important to understand for God provides a righteousness that is a declaration of righteousness through His Son Jesus Christ. "For he who has died is **freed**[11] from sin" (Romans 6:7). ὁ γὰρ ἀποθανὼν **δεδικαίωται**[12] ἀπὸ τῆς ἁμαρτίας. The word 'freed' means to declare and treat as righteous, that is right with God. All men are born in Adam, are not right with God and are in need of His provided righteousness or acquittal. All those in Christ have His provided righteousness and that is what saves them from eternal damnation. "For if by the transgression of the one, death reigned through the one, much more <u>those who receive the abundance of grace and of the gift of righteousness will reign in life through the One, Jesus Christ</u>" (Romans 5:17). Again, Christ's provided righteousness from the cross has nothing to do with His attributes of deity, but He did give up the free use of His divine attributes though they were fully with Him as He is Jehovah, the Son of God (Col. 2:9).

Christ always had all the attributes of deity for He has always been the Son of God eternally. Even as a babe to an adult to the cross, He was and is fully God. Jesus is immutable as the true God (Heb. 13:8). There was never a time when Jesus was not the Son of God, for He is the true God and eternal life (1 John 5:20). Prior to the incarnation He was the Son of God. At the incarnation He was the Son of God. The charge against

---

[11] [UBS] **δικαιόω** put into a right relationship (with God); acquit, declare and treat as righteous; show or prove to be right; set free (Ac 13.38; Ro 6.7); **δικαιόω** ... δικαιόω *make free* or *pure* ... *be set free, made pure* ἀπό *from* ... ὁ ἀποθανὼν δεδικαίωται ἀπὸ τ. ἁμαρτίας *the one who died is freed from sin* Ro 6:7. William Arndt et al., <u>A Greek-English Lexicon of the New Testament and Other Early Christian Literature : A Translation and Adaption of the Fourth Revised and Augmented Edition of Walter Bauer's Griechisch-Deutsches Worterbuch Zu Den Schrift En Des Neuen Testaments Und Der Ubrigen Urchristlichen Literatur</u> (Chicago: University of Chicago Press, 1979), 197–198. **δε-δικαίωται** perfect passive -αιόω, passive voice *be acquitted/freed* from the claims of sin. Max Zerwick and Mary Grosvenor, <u>A Grammatical Analysis of the Greek New Testament</u> (Rome: Biblical Institute Press, 1974), 472.

[12] See above footnote

Him for crucifixion was that He claimed to be the Son of God. "The Jews answered him, we have a law, and by that law He ought to die because He made Himself out *to be* the Son of God" (John 19:7). On the cross He never ceased to be the Son of God and He never ceased to be the perfect Son of man. What a Savior God has given us sealed with love (John 3:16).

Man needs to be right or righteous with God. Man is not right with God until he believes the gospel or good news concerning His Son. "Now I make known to you, brethren, the gospel which I preached to you, which also you received, in which also you stand, by which also you are saved, if you hold fast the word which I preached to you, unless you believed in vain. For I delivered to you as of first importance what I also received, that Christ died for our sins according to the Scriptures, and that He was buried, and that He was raised on the third day according to the Scriptures" (1 Cor. 15:1-4). The gospel is all about Jesus Christ. It is not what man does for he is already dead with God spiritually and condemned. Man can offer nothing to God but dead works for he is dead spiritually, bankrupt, and totally depraved[13] (Rom. 1:28). He can offer

---

[13] "The Bible further teaches with complete unanimity that the race is depraved—apart from the saving grace of God—and it is equally evident that no time can be indicated when this came to pass other than the fall of man in the Garden of Eden. The claim that the unregenerate are totally depraved is resented by many and for want of a right understanding of its meaning. If, as viewed by men, it is asserted that there is nothing good in man, the statement is untrue; for, as man is quick to declare, there is no human being so degraded that there is not some good in him. If, on the other hand, as viewed by God, it is claimed that man is without merit in His sight, the case is far different. Depravity as a doctrine does not stand or fall on the ground of man's estimation of himself; it rather reflects God's estimation of man." Lewis Sperry Chafer, *Systematic Theology*, vol. 2 (Grand Rapids, MI: Kregel Publications, 1993), 218–219. "The minds of unbelievers are depraved, hostile to God, blinded, and corrupt (Rom. 1:28; 8:6–7; 2 Cor. 4:4; Phil. 3:19; 1 Tim. 6:5; Titus 1:15). The unsaved do not acknowledge their sin and receive Christ as their Savior apart from God's written revelation, the Bible (1 Pet. 1:23), and the convicting and regenerating work of the Holy Spirit (John 16:8–11; Titus 3:5)" Roy B. Zuck, "Review of The Death of Truth Edited by Dennis McCallum and Postmodern Times by Gene Edward

nothing to God but filthy rags.

But, God has provided the way by His Son and only by His Son. It is all locked up in the Eternal Son and His body and His blood, the God-man. Nothing else will suffice, for God has provided the only righteous way by His righteous Son, and this via His cross (John 14:6).

The righteousness which God provides for all men can only be received by faith. Faith does not save but faith is the conduit by which one receives the free gift of His righteousness which does save. "But <u>the free gift</u> is not like the transgression. For if by the transgression of the one the many died (*all died*),[14] much more did the grace of God and the gift by the grace of the one Man, Jesus Christ, abound to the many[15] (*all*). And the gift is not like *that which came* through the one who sinned; for on the one hand <u>the judgment</u> *arose* <u>from one</u> *transgression* <u>resulting in condemnation</u>, but on the other hand the <u>free gift</u> *arose* from many transgressions <u>resulting in justification</u>. For if by the transgression of the one, death reigned through the one, **much more those who receive the abundance of grace and of the gift of righteousness** will reign in life through the One, Jesus Christ. So then as through one transgression <u>there resulted condemnation</u> **to all men**, even so through one act of righteousness <u>there resulted justification of life</u> **to all men**" (Rom 5:15-18).

Note well what Paul has stressed with these verses. As all men are condemned in the one transgression of Adam "even so through one act of righteousness <u>there resulted justification of life</u> **to all men**" (5:18). There is absolutely no problem here for this is speaking of unlimited atonement, not universal salvation. The Text makes it very clear that for one to reign in life (eternal life) through the One Jesus Christ, it is for "those

---

Veith," ed. Lin M. Williams, *Bibliotheca Sacra* 155 (1998): 116.

[14] οἱ πολλοί not "many" but *all* (who are many), the fact of a great number being more prominent to the Semitic mind than the fact of totality, cf Mt 20:28. Max Zerwick and Mary Grosvenor, <u>A Grammatical Analysis of the Greek New Testament</u> (Rome: Biblical Institute Press, 1974), 470.

[15] See previous footnote.

who receive the abundance of grace and of the gift of righteousness." These are the ones who will reign in life through the God-man, Jesus Christ. As all men are fully condemned in Adam, to have eternal life one must receive the gracious free given gift of righteousness. One receives this gift by faith, and again Scripture teaches faith does not save; only His grace saves. Men are only saved by His grace. It is all about Jesus not anything we do such as promises, commitments, making Him Lord, and all that is merely filthy rags. God calls on all men to believe in His Son. The question God asks all men is what will you do with my Son? Charles Spurgeon said it so well.

> *"Looking unto Jesus." — Hebrews 12:2,* It is ever the Holy Spirit's work to turn our eyes away from self to Jesus; but Satan's work is just the opposite of this, for he is constantly trying to make us regard ourselves instead of Christ. He insinuates, "Your sins are too great for pardon; you have no faith; you do not repent enough; you will never be able to continue to the end; you have not the joy of his children; you have such a wavering hold of Jesus." All these are thoughts about self, and we shall never find comfort or assurance by looking within. But the Holy Spirit turns our eyes entirely away from self: he tells us that we are nothing, but that "Christ is all in all." Remember, therefore, it is not *thy hold* of Christ that saves thee—it is Christ; it is not *thy joy* in Christ that saves thee—it is Christ; **it is not even faith in Christ, though that be the instrument—it is Christ's blood and merits; therefore, look not so much to thy hand with which thou art grasping Christ, as to Christ; look not to thy hope, but to Jesus, the source of thy hope; look not to thy faith, but to Jesus, the author and finisher of thy faith.** We shall never find happiness by looking at our prayers, our doings, or our feelings; it is what *Jesus* is, not what we are, that gives rest to the soul. If we would at once overcome Satan and have peace with God, it must be by "looking unto Jesus." Keep thine eye simply on him; let his death, his sufferings, his merits, his glories, his intercession, be fresh upon thy mind; when thou wakest in the morning look to him; when thou liest down at night look to him. Oh! let not thy hopes or fears come between thee and Jesus; follow hard after him, and he will never fail thee. "My hope is built on nothing less Than Jesus' blood and righteousness: I dare not trust

the sweetest frame, But wholly lean on Jesus' name."[16]

The question is how God accomplished all this on His Son's cross. The answer is He did it all with love by means of the last Adam (John 3:16). The great Creator of everything humbled Himself unto death. He became the last Adam, the Savior of all men. Paul wrote such great truth concerning Him and His humiliation. "He made Him who knew no sin *to be* sin on our behalf, that we might become the righteousness of God in Him" (2 Corinthians 5:21). He never sinned or became sinful. He did become the sin offering that men may be made righteous in Him. The last Adam did this by the blood of His cross.

His cross

"He was despised and forsaken of men, A man of sorrows, and acquainted with grief; and like one from whom men hide their face, He was despised, and we did not esteem Him. (Is. 53:3)

"Have this attitude in yourselves which was also in Christ Jesus, who, although He existed in the form of God, did not regard equality with God a thing to be grasped, but emptied Himself, taking the form of a bond-servant, *and* being made in the likeness of men. And being found in appearance as a man, He humbled Himself by becoming obedient to the point of death, even death on a cross. Therefore also God highly exalted Him, and bestowed on Him the name which is above every name, that at the name of Jesus every knee should bow, of those who are in heaven, and on earth, and under the earth, and that every tongue should confess that Jesus Christ is Lord, to the

---

[16]Spurgeon, C. H. (2006). *Morning and evening : Daily readings* (Complete and unabridged; New modern edition.) (June 28 AM). Peabody, MA: Hendrickson Publishers.

glory of God the Father" (Phil. 2:5-11).

Believers are continually to have a Christ like attitude which concentrates entirely on His humiliation. "Have this attitude[17] in yourselves which was also in Christ Jesus, who, although He existed in the form of God, did not regard equality with God a thing to be grasped" [18] (Phil. 2:5-6). 'Have this attitude' or have this thinking or mindset is a present imperative which may be hard to comprehend. It is almost impossible to comprehend how the Creator, the God of all glory could step down from His infinite position in glory and enter into His own finite creation as a man literally in human flesh yet without sin.

Jesus was always God and never ceased to be God even on the cross. As an infant, He could have spoken His own creation out of existence as well as He spoke it into existence. He could have done the same from the cross. As the Son of God, the second person of the triune Godhead, Jesus (God incarnate) was always in the form of God and could be nothing less. It is almost impossible for man to comprehend this 'attitude or thinking' that is how He stepped down to become man, to be hated, to be spit on, to be beaten, to be rejected, to become a sin offering and a curse, and finally to die for all

---

[17] Τοῦτο φρονεῖτε ἐν ὑμῖν ὃ καὶ ἐν Χριστῷ Ἰησοῦ, ὃς ἐν μορφῇ θεοῦ ὑπάρχων οὐχ ἁρπαγμὸν ἡγήσατο τὸ εἶναι ἴσα θεῷ. φρονέω ... to have an opinion with regard to something... to develop an attitude based on careful thought, *be minded/disposed* τοῦτο φρονεῖτε ἐν ὑμῖν ὃ καὶ ἐν Χριστῷ Ἰησοῦ *let the same kind of thinking dominate you as dominated Christ Jesus* Phil 2:5 (Christ went so far as to devoid himself of his divine status for the benefit of humanity; William Arndt, Frederick W. Danker, and Walter Bauer, <u>A Greek-English Lexicon of the New Testament and Other Early Christian Literature</u> (Chicago: University of Chicago Press, 2000), 1066.

[18] Τοῦτο φρονεῖτε ἐν ὑμῖν ὃ καὶ ἐν Χριστῷ Ἰησοῦ, ὃς ἐν μορφῇ θεοῦ ὑπάρχων οὐχ ἁρπαγμὸν ἡγήσατο τὸ εἶναι ἴσα θεῷ. ἁρπαγμός , οῦ, ὁ (rare in nonbiblical Greek; not found at all in the Greek translation of the Old Testament; ... only in Phil 2:6)... a violent seizure of property, *robbery* ... As equal to ἅρπαγμα, something to which one can claim or assert title by gripping or grasping.. William Arndt, Frederick W. Danker, and Walter Bauer, <u>A Greek-English Lexicon of the New Testament and Other Early Christian Literature</u> (Chicago: University of Chicago Press, 2000), 133–134.

men's sin. There was great continual suffering on the sin bearer. "But I have a baptism to undergo, and how distressed[19] I am until it is accomplished!" (Luke 12:50). From His birth or incarnation, death on the cross was always before Him. But this was not a normal death in any manner, for His coming death was for the punishment and guilt of sins for the world of sinful men. That is from the first Adam to the last man born in this world. Scriptures teach unlimited atonement and absolutely nothing else.

The last Adam came down from glory to do the Father's will which was perfectly His own will as the Son of man. There was never a conflict with the 'will' of the Son of man and the Father. With the God-man there was perfect meeting of the will.

There are three verses which should be noted. All the following verses are in the first class condition, which means there was no condition or contingency being presented by the prayer/s of the Son to the Father. He was not praying to the Father saying 'if' as a condition perhaps of avoiding the cross. If there were another way, tell Me. This is not what is being prayed about in any sense. The expression 'If it is possible' or better 'since this is possible' leaves the decision in the Father's hands or will.

> "And He went a little beyond *them*, and fell on His face and prayed, saying, **My Father, if it is possible**, let this cup pass from Me; yet not as I will, but as Thou wilt" (Mat 26:39) καὶ προελθὼν

---

[19]βάπτισμα δὲ ἔχω βαπτισθῆναι, καὶ πῶς **συνέχομαι** ἕως ὅτου τελεσθῇ. **συνέχομαι** verb indicative present passive 1st person singular from **συνέχω** … **to cause distress by force of circumstances,** *seize, attack, distress, torment* …πῶς συνέχομαι *how great is my distress, what vexation I must endure* **Lk 12:50.** The apostle, torn between conflicting emotions, says συνέχομαι ἐκ τῶν δύο *I am hard pressed* (to choose) *between the two* **Phil 1:23.** William Arndt, Frederick W. Danker, and Walter Bauer, *A Greek-English Lexicon of the New Testament and Other Early Christian Literature* (Chicago: University of Chicago Press, 2000), 970–971.

μικρὸν ἔπεσεν ἐπὶ πρόσωπον αὐτοῦ προσευχόμενος καὶ λέγων· πάτερ μου, εἰ δυνατόν ἐστιν, παρελθάτω ἀπ' ἐμοῦ τὸ ποτήριον τοῦτο· **πλὴν οὐχ ὡς ἐγὼ θέλω ἀλλ' ὡς σύ.**

"And He was saying, **Abba! Father! All things are possible for Thee**; remove this cup from Me; **yet not what I will, but what Thou wilt**" (Mark 14:36) καὶ ἔλεγεν· αββα ὁ πατήρ, πάντα δυνατά σοι· παρένεγκε τὸ ποτήριον τοῦτο ἀπ' ἐμοῦ· **ἀλλ' οὐ τί ἐγὼ θέλω ἀλλὰ τί σύ.**

"Saying, **Father, if Thou art willing**, remove this cup from Me; **yet not My will, but Thine be done**" (Luke 22:42) λέγων· πάτερ, εἰ βούλει παρένεγκε τοῦτο τὸ ποτήριον ἀπ' ἐμοῦ· **πλὴν μὴ τὸ θέλημά μου ἀλλὰ τὸ σὸν γινέσθω.**

What is presented here is that Jesus confirmed His will is the Father's will, and the Father's will is His will. The first Adam did not do the Father's will; the last Adam conformed to the Father's will flawlessly. All that Jesus wanted was for the Father's will to be done in His life which was proven by His very words (Mat. 26:39; Mark 14:36; Luke 22:42).

It must be noted that the true humanity of Christ would and did suffer almost infinitely under the shear agony of the guilt and punishment of all men's sin. Christ was about to face the penalty for all sin essentially in His humanity (Luke 12:50). It must be remembered that He is one person with two full natures, deity and human. His true humanity is crying out to His Father.

He was to die for all the punishment for all men's sin going back to Adam and all future sin of all mankind. He came to do the Father's will. "Therefore, when He comes into the world, He says, Sacrifice and offering Thou hast not desired, but a body Thou hast prepared for Me; In whole burnt offerings and *sacrifices* for sin Thou hast taken no pleasure. Then I said, 'Behold, I have come (In the roll of the book it is written of Me) To do Thy will, O God" (Heb. 10:5-7). He came to do the Father's will not to oppose it in any way, or to have the Father's will removed, changed, or modified by some prayer. Yet there was such great agony in the garden, perhaps more than that of the cross in a physical death. He would feel the agony of eternal separation in a moment in His humanity yet never being separated from God for He is God. Christ remained a perfectly righteous sacrifice with all the wrath of God coming on Him for our sins "One who has been tempted in all things as *we are, yet* without sin" (Heb 4:15). His suffering for all men's sin was more than any human could possibly bear. His prayer in the garden was acknowledging that even with all the ignominy and shame of the cross, He was in the Father's will for He only wanted the Father's will to be done.

> "We must note that from the first word of the prayer to the last Jesus submits to his Father's will. Even a mere supposition of not doing so is foreign to his soul. The true humanity of Jesus is revealed by these prayers; it had to be thus revealed because his entire passion was undergone by way of his human nature. The word 'cup' is here used figuratively and does not refer only to contents but to bitter, burning, deadly contents. 'If it is possible' leaves the decision in regard to that to the Father. The condition is one of reality and assumes that, if such a possibility existed, the Father would avail himself of it. Back of the brief condition lies the thought, 'if it is possible to redeem the world without drinking this horrible cup of death and wrath' then relieve me of this cup. 'Let it pass from me' means 'Do not put it to my lips.' With πλὴν 'nevertheless' Jesus implies, 'whatever may be involved in this possibility.' Although in his agony Jesus has mentioned the possibility, he really intends to yield everything to his Father's will and to put aside his own will. It is the human will of Jesus that speaks here. The agony suffered in Gethsemane will always bear an element of mystery for us because of the mystery involved in the union of Christ's two natures. For one thing, we have no conception of what sin, curse, wrath, death meant for the holy human nature of Jesus. Because he was sinless, he should not die; and yet because he was sinless and holy, he willed to die for our sin. The death of Jesus was far different from that of the courageous martyrs; they died after Jesus' death had removed their sin and guilt, the sting had been removed from the death through Christ's death, but Jesus died under sin and its curse, the sting of death tortured him with all its damnable power. The world's sin had, indeed, been assumed

by Jesus during his whole life, but here in Gethsemane the final moment of that assumption had come: with the coming of Judas and his band Jesus now actually stepped into the death that would expiate the world's sin."[20]

He humbled Himself by becoming the last Adam, the greatest servant of all to die for men's sin. He did not 'grasp or seize' this title of divinity as something to hold onto and exhibit continually. The great Creator became the Savior of all men for all sin for all time. He humbled Himself as the last Adam unto death. "But emptied Himself, taking the form of a bond-servant, *and* being made in the likeness of men. And being found in appearance as a man, He humbled Himself by becoming obedient to the point of death, even death on a cross"[21] (Phil. 2:7-8). He emptied Himself not of deity for that would not be possible. Jesus was always God in bodily form. "For in Him all the fullness of Deity dwells in bodily form" (Col. 2:9). He gave up the free use of His attributes, although they were all still very much with Him as the God-man. The great Creator stepped down from His glory to become the God-man. The last Adam was 100% God and 100% man, the literal God-man. That can never change even on the cross unto death. The great Creator humbled Himself taking the form or nature of man and entered His own creation as a man, the God-man, the last Adam.

---

[20] R. C. H. Lenski, *The Interpretation of St. Matthew's Gospel* (Minneapolis, MN: Augsburg Publishing House, 1964), 1039-1040.

[21] ἀλλὰ ἑαυτὸν **ἐκένωσεν** μορφὴν δούλου λαβών, ἐν ὁμοιώματι ἀνθρώπων γενόμενος· καὶ σχήματι εὑρεθεὶς ὡς ἄνθρωπος [UBS] **κενόω** deprive of power, make of no meaning or effect; ἐμαυτὸν κ. give up or lay aside what one possesses "**κενόω to make empty,** *to empty*…of divestiture of position or prestige: of Christ, who gave up the appearance of his divinity and took on the form of a slave, ἑαυτὸν ἐκένωσεν *he emptied himself, divested himself of his prestige* or *privileges* **Phil 2:7**" William Arndt, Frederick W. Danker, and Walter Bauer, <u>A Greek-English Lexicon of the New Testament and Other Early Christian Literature</u> (Chicago: University of Chicago Press, 2000), 539.

"The word translated **nature** (*morphē*) in verses 6 and 7 is a crucial term in this passage. This word (translated "form" in the KJV and NASB) stresses the inner essence or reality of that with which it is associated (cf. Mark 16:12). Christ Jesus, Paul said, is of the very essence (*morphē*) of God, and in His incarnation He embraced perfect humanity. His complete and absolute deity is here carefully stressed by the apostle. The Savior's claim to deity infuriated the Jewish leaders (John 5:18) and caused them to accuse Him of blasphemy (John 10:33). Though possessing full deity (John 1:14; Col. 2:9), Christ did not consider His **equality with God** (Phil. 2:6) as **something to be grasped** or held onto. In other words Christ did not hesitate to set aside His self-willed use of deity when He became a man. As God He had all the rights of deity, and yet during His incarnate state He surrendered His right to manifest Himself visibly as the God of all splendor and glory. Christ's humiliation included His making **Himself nothing**, taking the **very nature** (*morphē*) **of a servant**, and **being made in human likeness** (v. 7). These statements indicate that Christ became a man, a true human being. The words "made Himself nothing" are, literally, "He emptied Himself." "Emptied," from the Greek *kenoō*, points to the divesting of His self-interests, but not of His deity. "The very nature of a servant" certainly points to His lowly and humble position, His willingness to obey the Father, and serve others. He became a man, a true human being. "Likeness" suggests similarity but difference. Though His humanity was genuine, He was different from all other humans in that He was sinless (Heb. 4:15). Thus it is seen that Christ, while retaining the essence of God, was also human. In His incarnation He was *fully* God and *fully* man at the same time. He was God manifest in human flesh (John 1:14). Some have wrongly taught that the phrase, **being found in appearance as a man** (Phil. 2:8), means that He only *looked* human. But this contradicts verse 7. "Appearance" is the Greek *schēmati*, meaning an outer appearance which may be temporary. This contrasts with *morphē* ("very nature") in verses 6 and 7, which speaks of an outer appearance that reveals permanent inner quality. The condescension of Christ included not only His birth—the Incarnation in which He became the God-Man—but also His **death**. And it was the most cruel and despicable form of death—**even death on a cross!** (v. 8) This form of capital punishment was limited to non-Romans and the worst criminals. No better example of humiliation and a selfless attitude for believers to follow could possibly be given than that of Christ. With this example before them, the saints at Philippi should be "like-minded" (v. 2) and live humbly before their God and each other."[22]

Was Christ ever truly forsaken by God the Father? Part of Psalm 22 is quoted from the cross. One has to look at the whole Psalm to find out if this is truth.

- "My God, my God, why hast Thou forsaken me? Far from my deliverance are the words of my groaning" (Ps. 22:1).
- "And about the ninth hour Jesus cried out with a loud voice, saying, "Eli, Eli, lama sabachthani?" that is, "My God, My God, why hast Thou forsaken Me?" (Mat. 27:46).
- "And at the ninth hour Jesus cried out with a loud voice, "Eloi, Eloi, lama sabachthani?" which is translated, "My God, My God, why hast Thou forsaken Me?" (Mark 15:34).

"My God, my God, why hast Thou forsaken me? Far from my deliverance are the words of my groaning. ² O my God, I cry by day, but Thou dost not answer; and by night, but I have no rest. ³ Yet Thou art holy, O Thou who art enthroned upon the praises of Israel. ⁴ In Thee our fathers trusted; they trusted, and Thou didst deliver them. ⁵ To Thee they cried out, and were delivered; In Thee they trusted, and were not disappointed. ⁶ But I am a worm, and not a man, a reproach of men, and despised by the people. ⁷ All who see me sneer at me; They separate with the lip, they wag the head, *saying*, ⁸ Commit *yourself* to the LORD; let Him deliver him; Let Him rescue him, because He delights in him" (Ps. 22:1-8).

---

[22] Robert P. Lightner, "Philippians," in *The Bible Knowledge Commentary: An Exposition of the Scriptures*, ed. J. F. Walvoord and R. B. Zuck, vol. 2 (Wheaton, IL: Victor Books, 1985), 653–654.

Was the Messiah ever forsaken or abandoned by God? There is no way God abandoned Him in any sense. Psalm 22 indicates just the opposite. While this Psalm may be totally prophetic, it seems it was a Psalm of David which he penned or sang at a time of great suffering or agony. David may have felt abandoned or forsaken by God, but this was not true. Psalm 22 reflects a man crying out to God for help in a time of unbelievable crisis. Haven't we all been in unreal crises? Haven't we all wondered where God was or is at very trying times? Christ is on the cross literally facing the sinner's death because of all men's sin as He was taking on the full wrath of God against all sin. He became the guilt and sin offering that all men need in their place. The guilt of sin is being judged and taken away so a man may become not guilty, but righteous. The transaction on the cross we may never know, but one thing is certain He became the guilt offering for all men for all sin (Is. 53:10). Scripture is infinitely clear with this truth.

Note well that David, the sweet Psalmist of Israel, crying out to God for help knowing He is holy, can be trusted, and never disappoints. In fact, the truth is "Thou who art enthroned upon the praises of Israel" and these praises are not just some mindless praise but thanks and praises for His answer to the prayers of the people. The great Psalmist of Israel understood this well (2 Sam. 23:1). David may have felt forsaken by God, but he never was. Jesus may have felt forsaken but He never was.

> "David, apparently feeling forsaken by God and scoffed at by his enemies, was confident that God would not fully abandon him… Though sensing that God had forsaken him (v. 1), the psalmist drew renewed confidence from the fact that God had answered his ancestors' prayers (v. 4). David's initial cry, **My God, my God, why have You forsaken me?** is an expression appropriated by Christ on the cross (Matt. 27:46; Mark 15:34). God, whom David was addressing as "my God," had seemingly forsaken him. David prayed constantly (**by day** and **by night**) but there was no **answer**. 22:3. The confidence he mustered was from the knowledge that God answers prayer. God is **holy**, distinct from all the false gods of the

pagans in that He is alive and acts. In fact God is **enthroned…** and therefore received **praise** from the Israelites for answered prayer.22:4–5. David's ancestors, putting **their trust** in the Lord, prayed in their distress and were **delivered** by Him. So David was encouraged to keep on praying."[23]

Christ was calling out from the cross to God the Father Whom He loves and Who loves Him. Christ was never separated from the love of God. The last Adam i.e. the God-man took on the eternal punishment for the sins of the world. God never left Him for Jesus is God and the trinity can never be separated. The human nature was never separated from God or He would cease to be the Messiah. He never died spiritually for then He would have to be born again. On the cross was the God-man. He never ceased to be the God-man on the cross.

There was no separation until Christ died and then He went directly to the Father. His body went to the tomb for 3 days. The Father and the Son are eternally one and can never be separated. The triune Godhead is three Persons Who can never be separated as they are eternally one. If they were ever separated there would be more than one God. The Father and the Son are always one in all essence.

> "The three Persons are seen achieving the creation of the universe. To each this vast work is accredited separately and with the implication that each acted alone and when so acting was wholly sufficient and responsible. In the greater work of redemption—specifically the sufferings and death of Christ—it is the Son who suffers and dies, but the Father gives the Son and the Son is offered by the Eternal Spirit. Here is revealed the deepest unified action and cooperation. The Son cries, "My God, my God, why hast thou forsaken me?" (Ps. 22:1; Matt. 27:46), yet it is affirmed that it was the very God to whom He cried that was, at that precise moment, "in Christ, reconciling the world unto himself" (2 Cor. 5:19). To finite minds all this is paradoxical, yet it serves to emphasize anew the deeper truth that, though there are three Persons in the Godhead, there is but one

---

[23] Allen P. Ross, "Psalms," in *The Bible Knowledge Commentary: An Exposition of the Scriptures*, ed. J. F. Walvoord and R. B. Zuck, vol. 1 (Wheaton, IL: Victor Books, 1985), 810.

essence. Neither the Father nor the Spirit became incarnate. The action of the Son was always according to the will of the Father and never more so than in His death (Phil. 2:8). All the Son wrought was in the power of the Spirit and never more perfectly than in His death. Objectively, not only did the Father *give* the Son (John 3:16), but He *sent* the Son (John 3:17), He *loved* the Son (John 3:35), He is *glorified* in the Son (John 14:13), and He *glorified* the Son (Acts 3:13); yet wholly consonant is this truth with a deeper reality, namely, that the Father and the Son are one (John 10:30; 14:9–11; 17:21)."[24]

When Jesus died there was a separation of His soul (immaterial) from His body. Physical death is a separation of the soul from the body. But no man took His physical life or His spiritual life. Jesus never died spiritually for then He would cease to be a flawlessly infinite sacrifice for all sin for all men for all time. Again, if Jesus had died spiritually, He would have had to be born again which is impossible for He was always the God-man and He would cease to be the God-man.

Actually, no man could take Jesus life in any sense. He had to give up His own life of Himself yet He had the power also to resurrect Himself. "For this reason the Father loves Me, because I lay down My life that I may take it again. No one has taken it away from Me, but I lay it down on My own initiative. I have authority to lay it down, and I have authority to take it up again. This commandment I received from My Father" (John 10:17).

He laid down His life of His own free will. Note the way John describes His departure or His death, yet departure might be better. "When Jesus therefore had received the sour wine, He said, it is finished! And He bowed His head, and gave up His spirit" (John 19:30). Note the reversal here as most people die and then bow their head, this was not so with Christ.

> "The sixth word or saying that **Jesus** spoke from the cross was the single Greek work *tetelestai* which means **It is finished**. Papyri receipts for taxes have been recovered with the word *tetelestai* written

---

[24] Lewis Sperry Chafer, *Systematic Theology*, vol. 3 (Grand Rapids, MI: Kregel Publications, 1993), 53.

across them, meaning "paid in full." This word on Jesus' lips was significant. When He said, "It is finished" (not "I am finished"), He meant His redemptive work was completed. He had been made sin for people (2 Cor. 5:21) and had suffered the penalty of God's justice which sin deserved. Even in the moment of His death, Jesus remained the One who gave up His life (cf. John 10:11, 14, 17–18). **He bowed His head** (giving His seventh saying, "Father, into Your hands I commit My spirit" [Luke 23:46]) **and** then dismissed **His spirit**. This differs from the normal process in death by crucifixion in which the life-spirit would ebb away and then the head would slump forward."[25]

The last Adam was raised from the dead by the Father, the Son, and the Holy Spirit. Not only was the triune Godhead involved with the creation, they were all involved with the greatest miracle ever, the resurrection of Jesus Christ. The entire Christian faith rests on the Person of Christ and His work on the cross. His resurrection verifies the entire inerrant written Word of God and the living Word of God, the last Adam. The entire trinity is confirming this truth.

- "Paul, an apostle not *sent* from men, nor through the agency of man, but through Jesus Christ, and God the Father, who raised Him from the dead" (Gal 1:1)
- "But if the Spirit of Him who raised Jesus from the dead dwells in you, He who raised Christ Jesus from the dead will also give life to your mortal bodies through His Spirit who indwells you" (Rom 8:11)
- "Jesus answered and said to them, "Destroy this temple, and in three days I will raise it up." [20] The Jews therefore said, "It took forty-six years to build this temple, and will You raise it up in three days?" [21] But He was

---

[25] Edwin A. Blum, "John," in *The Bible Knowledge Commentary: An Exposition of the Scriptures*, ed. J. F. Walvoord and R. B. Zuck, vol. 2 (Wheaton, IL: Victor Books, 1985), 340.

speaking of the temple of His body" (John 2:19-21).

The resurrection of Jesus Christ verifies everything concerning Him. "*He* who was delivered up because of our transgressions, and was raised because of our justification" (Romans 4:25).[26]

> "Mentioning the Lord Jesus led Paul to state again the Savior's central place in God's program of providing righteousness for sinful people by grace through faith. Both Christ's death and His resurrection are essential to that work of justification. **He was delivered over** (by God the Father; cf. 8:32) **to death for our sins** (lit., "on account of or because of" [*dia* with the accusative] "our trespasses" [*paraptōmata*, "false steps"; cf. 5:15, 17, 20; Eph. 2:1]). Though not a direct quotation, these words in substance are taken from Isaiah 53:12 (cf. Isa. 53:4–6). Also He **was raised to life for** ("on account of" or "because of" [*dia* with the accusative]) **our justification**. Christ's death as God's sacrificial Lamb (cf. John 1:29) was to pay the redemptive price for the sins of all people (Rom. 3:24) so that God might be free to forgive those who respond by faith to that provision. Christ's resurrection was the proof (or demonstration and vindication) of God's acceptance of Jesus' sacrifice (cf. 1:4). Thus because He lives, God can credit His provided righteousness to the account of every person who responds by faith to that offer. In chapter 4, Paul presented several irrefutable reasons why justification is by faith: (1) Since justification is a gift, it cannot be earned by works (vv. 1–8). (2) Since Abraham was justified before he was circumcised, circumcision has no relationship to justification (vv. 9–12). (3) Since Abraham was justified centuries before the Law, justification is not based on the Law (vv. 13–17). (4) Abraham was justified because of his faith in God, not because of his works (vv. 18–25).[27]

If Christ was not raised from the dead then all concerning Him is worthless. It would mean the Word of God was not true

---

[26] ὃς παρεδόθη διὰ τὰ παραπτώματα ἡμῶν καὶ ἠγέρθη διὰ τὴν δικαίωσιν ἡμῶν.
[27] John A. Witmer, "Romans," in *The Bible Knowledge Commentary: An Exposition of the Scriptures*, ed. J. F. Walvoord and R. B. Zuck, vol. 2 (Wheaton, IL: Victor Books, 1985), 455.

and we have no Savior. "And if Christ has not been raised, then our preaching is vain, your faith also is vain" (1 Cor. 15:14). But, Jesus has been raised from the dead, the resurrection of the dead which no other faith, religion, belief system, etc. has. All the other prophets of all other faiths are quite dead. Christ has been raised from the dead verifying all truth concerning God's Word and Himself.

His priesthood

"For it was fitting that we should have such a high priest, holy, innocent, undefiled, separated from sinners and exalted above the heavens" (Heb. 7:26)

"And behold, the veil of the temple was torn in two from top to bottom, and the earth shook; and the rocks were split, (Mat 27:51). The moment Christ died the veil was torn in two and this can only be by God. "The veil of the temple was torn in two from top to bottom: The temple had two veils or curtains—one in front of the holy place and the other separating the holy place from the Most Holy Place. It was the second of these that was torn, demonstrating that God had opened up access to Himself through His Son (see Heb. 6:19; 10:19-22). Only God could have torn the veil from the top."[28]

The way to God changed at Christ's last breath or death. The law ended or was fulfilled.

"For Christ is the end of the law for righteousness to everyone who believes" (Rom. 10:4). "But when Christ appeared[29] *as* a

---

[28] The Nelson Study Bible, Nelson Ministry Services Special Edition, Thomas Nelson Publishers, Nashville, 1997, p. 1632.

[29] **παραγενόμενος** verb participle aorist middle nominative masculine singular from **παραγίνομαι** [UBS] **παραγίνομαι** (aor. παρεγενόμην, subj. παραγένωμαι) come, arrive; appear; come to one's defense, stand by (2 Tm 4.16). The root word has the meaning of come or arrives; and with the aorist participle the normal rendering would have the meaning of has come or has arrived. Perhaps when Christ came or arrived He entered…

high priest of the good things to come, *He entered* through the greater and more perfect tabernacle, not made with hands, that is to say, not of this creation" (Heb. 9:11). Christ arrived as the high priest and entered the true and perfect tabernacle. This is the true tabernacle which is in heaven.[30] The writer of Hebrews has emphasized this truth several times to the readers. He wanted them to fully understand that Christ is now functioning as the true high priest in the true tabernacle. He is the great high priest of the order of Meldchizedek.

> "Now the main point in what has been said *is this*: <u>we have such a high priest</u>, who has taken His seat at the right hand of the throne of the Majesty in the heavens, a minister in the sanctuary, and in the true tabernacle, which the Lord pitched, not man. For every high priest is appointed to offer both gifts and sacrifices; hence it is necessary that this *high priest* also have something to offer. Now if He were on earth, He would not be a priest at all, since there are those who offer the gifts according to the Law; who serve a copy and shadow of the heavenly things, just as Moses was warned *by God* when he was about to erect the tabernacle; for, "See," He says, "that you make all things according to the pattern which was shown you on the mountain" (Heb 8:1-5). "So also Christ did not glorify Himself so as to become a high priest, but He who said to Him, <u>Thou art My Son, Today I have begotten Thee;</u> [6] <u>just as He says also in another passage, Thou art a priest forever according to the order of Melchizedek</u>" (Heb. 5:5-6).

Melchizedek is mentioned 10 times in the Text and 7 times in the book of Hebrews. During this dispensation, there is no earthly priest. Believers have no earthly priest as their high priest is the Lord Jesus serving in the true temple in heaven. All believers are priests serving their high priest. The true priest is now mediating His new covenant in the true tabernacle. The last Adam is the acting high priest forever according to the order of Melchizedek. This was very important for these

---

[30] Some of the following commentary is taken from this author's books "The Greatness of His Blood and The New Covenant' and 'The Greatness of The Day of the Lord and Christ's Kingdom." There are some changes but for more information please see these resources.

Hebrew believers to understand as well as all believers. The Hebrew believers as well as any believers could not go back to the old system of law and its sacrifices, for they are fulfilled in Him and His perfect offering of Himself.

We have a great high priest who we can go to for help at any time. "For we do not have a high priest who cannot sympathize with our weaknesses, but One who has been tempted in all things as *we are, yet* without sin" (Heb 4:15). Did the Hebrew believers understand any of this? Do believers understand any of this? Does the church really understand going to their true high priest? Do they understand what the last Adam is doing now?

Christ is now ministering in the true tabernacle in heaven. His ministry is that of mediating His new covenant. "How much more will the blood of Christ, who through the eternal Spirit offered Himself without blemish to God, cleanse your conscience from dead works to serve the living God? And for this reason He is the mediator of a new covenant, in order that since a death has taken place for the redemption of the transgressions that were *committed* under the first covenant, those who have been called may receive the promise of the eternal inheritance" (Heb 9:14-15).

> "When Christ **entered the most holy place once for all by His own blood** (v. 12; cf. Christ's blood in v. 14; 10:19, 29; 13:20) rather than by animal blood, He likewise demonstrated the superiority of His service because His blood had **obtained eternal redemption**. Thus the value of His sacrifice is immeasurably greater than the animal offerings of the Levitical arrangements. A perfect ransom price had been paid for human "redemption," and because it need not be paid again (this sacrificial act was "once for all," *ephapax;* cf. 7:27; 10:10) that redemption is an "eternal" one. 9:13–14. This "eternal redemption" through which the blessings of the New Covenant (cf. 8:10–12) have reached all believers, should affect the way believers serve God. Old-Covenant rituals served for the **ceremonially unclean** and only made them **outwardly clean**. But **the blood of Christ** can do much more."[31]

---

[31] Hodges, Z. C. (1985). Hebrews. In J. F. Walvoord & R. B. Zuck (Eds.),

He in the office of the high priest of Melchizedek is now mediating the new covenant in the true tabernacle. Scripture is perfectly clear with this truth.

- "But now He has obtained a more excellent ministry, by as much as He is[32] also the **mediator of a better covenant**, which has been enacted on better promises" (Heb. 8:6).
- "And for this reason He is[33] the **mediator** of a new covenant, in order that since a death has taken place for the redemption of the transgressions that were *committed* under the first covenant, those who have been called may receive the promise of the eternal inheritance" (Hebrews 9:15).
- "And to Jesus, the **mediator**[34] of a new covenant, and to the sprinkled blood, which speaks better than *the blood* of Abel" (Hebrews 12:24).

The Bible Knowledge Commentary: An Exposition of the Scriptures (J. F. Walvoord & R. B. Zuck, Ed.) (Heb 9:11–14). Wheaton, IL: Victor Books.
[32] νυν[ὶ] δὲ διαφορωτέρας τέτυχεν λειτουργίας, ὅσῳ καὶ κρείττονός ἐστιν διαθήκης μεσίτης, ἥτις ἐπὶ κρείττοσιν ἐπαγγελίαις νενομοθέτηται. Note the ἐστιν which means 'he is' now mediator and continues as mediator.
[33] Καὶ διὰ τοῦτο διαθήκης καινῆς μεσίτης ἐστίν, ὅπως θανάτου γενομένου εἰς ἀπολύτρωσιν τῶν ἐπὶ τῇ πρώτῃ διαθήκῃ παραβάσεων τὴν ἐπαγγελίαν λάβωσιν οἱ κεκλημένοι τῆς αἰωνίου κληρονομίας Note the ἐστι which means 'he is' now mediator and continues as mediator. Note also 'new covenant' is emphasized in context being brought forward in the Text.
[34] καὶ διαθήκης νέας μεσίτῃ Ἰησοῦ καὶ αἵματι ῥαντισμοῦ κρεῖττον λαλοῦντι παρὰ τὸν Ἄβελ.
To Jesus (Ἰησου [*Iēsou*]). This great fact is not to be overlooked (Phil. 2:10f.). He is there as Lord and Saviour and still "Jesus." **The mediator of a new covenant** (διαθηκης νεας μεσιτη [*diathēkēs neas mesitēi*]). As already shown (7:22; 8:6, 8, 9, 10; 9:15) and now gloriously consummated. **To the blood of sprinkling** (αἵματι ραντισμου [*haimati rantismou*]). As in 9:19–28. **Than Abel** (παρα τον Ἄβελ [*para ton Abel*]). Accusative as in 1:4. **Better** (κρειττον [*kreitton*]). Comparative of καλος [*kalos*]. Abel's blood still speaks (11:4), but it is as nothing compared to that of Jesus. A.T. Robertson, *Word Pictures in the New Testament* (Nashville, TN: Broadman Press, 1933), Heb

"But Jesus' ministry surpasses that of the Levitical priests just as the covenant He mediates supersedes theirs. (The word **Mediator** is used of Jesus by the author three times—8:6; 9:15; 12:24.) The word **ministry** (*leitourgia*, cf. "serves," 8:2) again strikes the pivotal note, but it is now added that the superiority of the new priestly service is related to a superior covenant, which in turn **is founded on better promises**. Both the covenant and its promises will now be considered… That there is a promise of a New Covenant the writer will shortly prove by quoting Jeremiah 31:31–34. By doing so, he argued that such a promise demonstrates the inadequacy of the old one. 8:8–12. The promise of a New Covenant was made, the writer pointed out, in a passage where God **found fault with the people**. The Old Covenant failed because of the sinfulness of the nation, for which it had no remedy. The **New Covenant**, however, has such a remedy."[35] "Their consciences ought to be perfectly free from any need to engage in such things and, retaining their confidence in the perfect efficacy of the Cross, they should hold fast their profession and **serve the living God** within the New-Covenant arrangements. 9:15. To do so is to retain the hope of an **eternal inheritance** (cf. "eternal redemption" in v. 12 and "the eternal Spirit" in v. 14) which has been **promised** to recipients of New-Covenant life. **Christ is the Mediator** (cf. 8:6; 12:24) of that **covenant**, and the "inheritance" is available to **those who are called** since the death of the Mediator has freed them from all guilt derived **from the sins committed under the First Covenant**. The author was here perhaps countering the appeal of the sectarians, or others, to the "guilt feelings" of those Jewish Christians who must often have been charged with deserting their ancestral faith. But the blood of Christ ought to quiet their consciences permanently and lead them to pursue the "eternal inheritance" which the New-Covenant relationship brought them… The author has made it clear that Christ's death has instituted a better covenant (vv. 11–15) which is superior to animal offerings (vv. 12–14). But the need for such a sacrifice has yet to be explored. So a key word in this subunit is "necessary" (*anankē*, vv. 16, 23). In the process of exploring this point, the author clearly underscored the measureless superiority of the sacrificial death of Christ."[36] "The realities that pertain to New-Covenant people and to which they **have**

12:24.
[35] Zane C. Hodges, "Hebrews," in *The Bible Knowledge Commentary: An Exposition of the Scriptures*, ed. J. F. Walvoord and R. B. Zuck, vol. 2 (Wheaton, IL: Victor Books, 1985), 800.
[36] Ibid, 802.

come are even more impressive because they are **heavenly**. Not only is there the heavenly **city**, but there are also heaven-related beings, both **angels** and people, associated with it. The term **church of the firstborn** may mean the assembly of those whose inheritance rights are already won (since under the OT Law the "firstborn" was the primary heir; cf. v. 16). They have already gone on to the heavenly regions where the angels are. But above all, it is to **God, the Judge of all men**, that they have come—and there are some who indeed can stand His searching scrutiny of their lives (**the spirits of righteous men made perfect**; cf. 10:14; 11:40)—and **to Jesus the Mediator** (cf. 8:6; 9:15) **of a New Covenant** whose atoning **blood** does not cry for judgment as did Abel's but secures the acceptance of all New-Covenant persons. If the readers would contemplate these things properly, they would be awed by them and more inclined to fulfill their call to the highest privileges that the New Covenant can provide."[37]

The church not only celebrates the new covenant especially the blood of the new covenant for eternal life but also for its ministry of righteousness. "Who also made us adequate *as* servants of a new covenant, not of the letter, but of the Spirit; for the letter kills, but the Spirit gives life. But if the ministry of death, in letters engraved on stones, came with glory, so that the sons of Israel could not look intently at the face of Moses because of the glory of his face, fading *as* it was, how shall the ministry of the Spirit fail to be even more with glory? For if the ministry of condemnation has glory, much more does the ministry of righteousness abound in glory" (2 Cor. 3:6).

"Paul's emphasis on the **New Covenant** implies that his opponents were ministers of the Old Covenant. The Mosaic Covenant was a written revelation of the righteousness God asked of Israel (e.g., Ex. 19–23). It was accepted with an oath of obedience and a blood sacrifice (Ex. 24). When Israel proved unable and unwilling to remain faithful to that covenant, God graciously intervened and promised a New Covenant (Jer. 31:31–34; 32:40), new (*kainēs*) both in time and in quality. It was inaugurated by Christ in His sacrifice on the cross (Luke 22:20), and is entered into by faith (Phil. 3:9) and lived out in dependence on the Spirit (Rom. 7:6; 8:4). (However, the physical and national aspects of the New Covenant which pertain to

---

[37] Ibid, 811.

Israel have not been appropriated to the church. Those are yet to be fulfilled in the Millennium. The church today shares in the soteriological aspects of that covenant, established by Christ's blood for all believers [cf. Heb. 8:7–13].)"[38]

The apostles as well as the Church at Corinth were ministers of a new covenant. They were to be serving under their High Priest, the mediator of the new covenant. Their sufficiency was from God "Who also made us adequate *as* servants of <u>a new covenant</u>, not of the letter, but of the Spirit; for the letter kills, <u>but the Spirit gives life</u>" (2 Cor. 3:6). Paul was defining the nature of the ministry of the new covenant in contrast to ministry under the old covenant. They were servants of the new covenant.[39]

- servants of a new covenant (the only covenant that gives life is the new covenant)
- not of the letter (the letter of the law kills)
- but of the Spirit (they ministered by God's Holy Spirit)
- for the letter kills (the Mosaic law was a ministry of death)
- but the Spirit gives life (God the Holy Spirit gives life)

Paul clarifies the difference in ministry by contrasting the two ministries. "But if the ministry of death, in letters engraved on stones, came with glory, so that the sons of Israel

---

[38] David K. Lowery, "2 Corinthians," in *The Bible Knowledge Commentary: An Exposition of the Scriptures*, ed. J. F. Walvoord and R. B. Zuck, vol. 2 (Wheaton, IL: Victor Books, 1985), 560–561.

[39] **Who also made us sufficient for such confidence** (ὅς και ἱκανωσεν ἡμας [*hos kai hikanōsen hēmas*]). Late causative verb from ἱκανος [*hikanos*] (verse 5) first aorist active indicative, "who (God) rendered us fit." In N.T. only here and Col. 1:12. **As ministers of a new covenant** (διακονους καινης διαθηκης [*diakonous kainēs diathēkēs*]). Predicate accusative with ἱκανωσεν [*hikanōsen*]. For διαθηκη [*diathēkē*] see on Matt. 26:28 and for διακονος [*diakonos*] on Matt. 20:26 and for καινης [*kainēs*] (fresh and effective) on Luke 5:38. Only God can make us that. Robertson, A. (1933). *Word Pictures in the New Testament* (2 Cor. 3:6). Nashville, TN: Broadman Press.

could not look intently at the face of Moses because of the glory of his face, fading *as* it was, how shall the ministry of the Spirit fail to be even more with glory" (2 Cor. 3:7-8) Paul was not ministering condemnation through the law but the righteousness which only flows from Christ's blood of the new covenant providing eternal redemption and transformation (2 Cor. 3:18).[40]

This is very clear, emphatic, and in context. To say Paul was not ministering the new covenant misses the whole point of what he is discussing with the Corinthians. He is establishing the fact that his whole ministry was based on the new covenant and the righteousness which flows from it. "For if the ministry of condemnation has glory, much more does the ministry of righteousness abound in glory" (2 Cor. 3:9).

Note the dramatic contrast Paul is making between those who minister the law and those who minister the new covenant. Paul was concerned about those who were still ministering the old system, and this was what the Judaizers were doing (and many do today).

Paul and the apostles had the ministry of righteousness which flows from the new covenant. Paul had this confidence and he knew he and the other apostles were servants or ministers of the new covenant (3:9):

- For if the ministry of condemnation has glory=the Law
- much more does the ministry of righteousness abound in glory=the new covenant

Paul made it very clear that God made him and the other apostles ministers[41] of the new covenant. What the old covenant could not do, weak as it was through the flesh, God could do through the new covenant which imparts the life-giving Spirit.

---

[40] " But we all, with unveiled face beholding as in a mirror the glory of the Lord, are being transformed into the same image from glory to glory, just as from the Lord, the Spirit" (2Cor. 3:18).

[41] His ministry was based on the new covenant as was his salvation.

The last Adam, the high priest of the order of Melchizedek is mediating the new covenant especially His righteousness to eternal life.

The church is also a ministry of the new covenant. The church is not a ministry of the law but of His righteousness. "God declares righteous those who believe in His Son, and then the Holy Spirit empowers the believer to live righteously. This first work of God is called justification, and the second is called sanctification."[42] The dispensation of grace or the church age is rooted in the new covenant. The church celebrates the new covenant. Praise God for His blood of the new covenant. Praise God we have a great high priest.

> "Since then <u>we have a great high priest</u> who has passed through the heavens<u>, Jesus the Son of God, let us hold fast our confession</u>. [15] For we do not have a high priest who cannot sympathize with our weaknesses, but One who has been tempted in all things as *we are, yet* without sin" (Heb. 4:14-15). "And the Holy Spirit also bears witness to us; for after saying. [16] Let us therefore draw near with confidence to the throne of grace, that we may receive mercy and may find grace to help in time of need. (Heb. 4:14-16) This is the covenant that I will make with them after those days, says the Lord: I will put My laws upon their heart, And upon their mind I will write them, *He then says,* [17] And their sins and their lawless deeds I will remember no more.[18] Now where there is forgiveness of these things, <u>there is no longer *any* offering for sin</u>. [19]Since therefore, brethren, <u>we have confidence to enter the holy place by the blood of Jesus</u>, [20] by a new and living way which He inaugurated for us through the veil, that is, His flesh, [21] and since *we have* a great priest over the house of God" (Heb. 10:15-21).

Praise God for His blood of the new covenant. He is mediating the covenant in the true tabernacle in heaven as the high priest. The church should be celebrating our High Priest, the God-man, the last Adam and what He has done for us through His blood of His new covenant.

The last Adam is not only the acting High Priest of the

---

[42] The Nelson Study Bible, Nelson Ministry Services Special Edition, Thomas Nelson Publishers, Nashville, 1997, p.1948.

church that is His body; He is also coming to set up His covenanted kingdom.

His kingdom

> "I kept looking in the night visions, And behold, with the clouds of heaven One like a Son of Man was coming, And He came up to the Ancient of Days And was presented before Him. And to Him was given dominion, Glory and a kingdom, that all the peoples, nations, and *men of every* language Might serve Him. His dominion is an everlasting dominion which will not pass away; and His kingdom is one which will not be destroyed" (Dan. 7:13-14)[43]

The first Adam was given a rule or dominion at creation over the earth which began when God said "Let Us make man in Our image, according to Our likeness; <u>and let them rule</u> over the fish of the sea and over the birds of the sky and over the cattle and <u>over all the earth</u>, and over every creeping thing that creeps on the earth" (Gen. 1:26). Man was created to rule under and with God over this present creation which we know as earth. "And God created man in His own image, in the image of God He created him; male and female He created them. And God blessed them; and God said to them, Be fruitful and multiply, and fill the earth, and subdue[44] it; and rule over the fish of the sea and over the birds of the sky, and over every living thing that moves on the earth" (Gen. 1:27-28). Although

---

[43] It must be noted that the church is not the kingdom nor does the church bring in His kingdom. The kingdom is given to the Son of man by God the Father. The Son then returns to take His throne over Israel in Israel. For more information please refer to this author's 'The Greatness of the Day of the Lord and Christ's Kingdom.'

[44] כָּבַשׁ, ... subdue, bring into bondage ... *subdue, dominate*, the earth Gen 1:28. Francis Brown, Samuel Rolles Driver, and Charles Augustus Briggs, <u>Enhanced Brown-Driver-Briggs Hebrew and English Lexicon</u> (Oxford: Clarendon Press, 1977), 461.

under God, Adam and Eve were given complete dominion over everything on the planet but one tree (Gen. 2:16-17). The downfall of Adam and all men was that one tree, and by Adam eating all died in Adam. Adam and Eve had a God given free will of contrary free choice. They were not robots or puppets but had the free choice of choosing for God or against God. The free will of man will always chose the evil. The last Adam did only the will of the Father by choosing the good and understood the perfect fear of the Lord (Proverbs 8:13). The last Adam paid the price of all sin, primarily the first sin which condemned all men.

Adam and Eve were not only to rule over all the earth but to subdue it and multiply and fill the earth. Psalm 8 as well and other verses confirm this. "Thou dost make him to rule over the works of Thy hands; Thou hast put all things under his feet, all sheep and oxen, and also the beasts of the field, the birds of the heavens, and the fish of the sea, whatever passes through the paths of the seas" (Ps. 8:6-8). "God's purpose in creating human life in His image was functional: man is to **rule** or have dominion (1:26, 28). God's dominion was presented by a "representative."... However, because of sin all things are not under man's dominion (Heb. 2:8). But Jesus Christ will establish dominion over all the earth (Heb. 2:5–8) at His second coming. God pronounced His blessing on the **male and the female**: they were to **be fruitful and increase in number**. In Genesis, to be blessed was to be enriched and fertile. Such marvelous decrees of **God** would be significant for Israel which was God's representative on earth. She would enter the land of promise and would expect God's continued blessing."[45]

The last Adam Who is in the royal seed line of David will establish His kingdom on the earth. He will reign with perfect justice and righteousness, because the nature of His kingdom will be His justice and righteousness. Everyone needs His

---

[45] Allen P. Ross, "Genesis," in *The Bible Knowledge Commentary: An Exposition of the Scriptures*, ed. J. F. Walvoord and R. B. Zuck, vol. 1 (Wheaton, IL: Victor Books, 1985), 29.

righteousness just to enter His kingdom. "Behold, *the* days are coming, declares the LORD, When I shall raise up for David a righteous Branch; And He will reign as king and act wisely And do justice and righteousness in the land"[46] (Jer. 23:5). This verse does not refer to heaven and has nothing to do with heaven in any sense; this is His future covenanted kingdom on this present earth. His justice and righteousness will reign supreme on the earth. There is very little of this anywhere even in the church. This is why we are to seek this kingdom where righteousness dwells (Mat. 6:33). "But let justice roll down like waters And righteousness like an ever-flowing stream" (Amos 5:24). To say all or any of this is happening today anywhere, one has to be rather blind and get back to a study of His Word especially His covenants.

This kingdom was covenanted by God through the eternal, unilateral, unconditional covenants (the Abrahamic, Davidic, new, and land). God literally put Himself under contract to execute word for word what He has promised in the covenants. It is crucial to understand God's biblical covenants for they define His covenanted program for man on the earth. God has literally put Himself under contract. He has revealed Himself to man primarily by His inerrant Word and man is accountable to understand what God has revealed. God has revealed Himself and His purposes not in mystery enshrouded with secrecy, but in such a way that man is fully capable and responsible to comprehend what has been revealed.

It is impossible to miss in Scripture the *biblical* covenants that God has made with the elect Jewish nation of Israel. God never gave His Word, especially the biblical covenants, to deceive, but to be fully comprehended and understood. The Abrahamic, land, Davidic and new covenants are the fountainhead from which God totally defines His entire redemptive kingdom program. These eternal, unconditional,

---

[46] Note that the Hebrew word בָּאָרֶץ here can be 'in the land or in the earth." All this will flow from Jerusalem which will be the place of His dwelling and throne on earth among His people Israel forever (Ezek. 43:7).

unilateral covenants clearly reveal: the covenanted blessings, the covenanted people, the covenanted nation, the covenanted land, the covenanted seed, the covenanted house, the covenanted throne, the covenanted kingdom, the covenanted king, the covenanted reign, the covenanted redemption, the covenanted cleansing, the covenanted Spirit, and much more. Absolutely not one of these defines the church but blessings do flow from all the covenants to the church. The church is defined by Christ Himself (Mat. 16:13-20), not the biblical covenants. Even the apostles did not understand what the church truly was until sometime later (see Acts chapters 8 and 10). Paul kept preaching and teaching the coming kingdom (Acts 28:23-31).

All the biblical covenants when taken literally describe and clearly define but one covenanted people and nation and that is the Jewish nation Israel. All the biblical covenants if taken literally describe but one covenanted Jewish throne and kingdom. All the biblical covenants if taken literally describe a single unity of purpose and design. All the biblical books of the prophets and their prophecies, which ultimately flow from God's biblically covenanted program, describe but one covenanted Jewish throne and kingdom. All events in world history are heading toward His earthly covenanted kingdom characterized by His justice and His righteousness where all the nations will serve Him. "I kept looking in the night visions, And behold, with the clouds of heaven One like a Son of Man was coming, And He came up to the Ancient of Days And was presented before Him. And to Him was given dominion, Glory and a kingdom, that all the peoples, nations, and *men of every* language Might serve Him. His dominion is an everlasting dominion which will not pass away; and His kingdom is one which will not be destroyed" (Dan. 7:13-14). This kingdom will go into the eternal state which will be addressed.

Against the accusation of being too pedantic or too Jewish about the details of the biblical covenants, it must be remembered that Jesus as the Jewish Messiah (Christ) has His covenanted rule as the King described in detail by the biblical covenants.⁴⁷ This is what the Jewish throne and kingdom are all about. Jesus is the Jewish Messiah (the Christ), the Anointed One who must reign from David's throne over the restored Jewish kingdom with much more blessings. The biblical covenants must be literally and completely fulfilled, for Christ must reign in this identical theocratic kingdom for the covenants to be fulfilled. The church is not a Jewish kingdom with a Jewish throne in a covenanted land. God changed nothing, or if He has, then He has done violence to His own Word.

This is why there is Christ's command to seek⁴⁸ His kingdom first (Mat. 6:33; Luke 12:31). This is His coming kingdom which His disciples were taught to pray for (Mat. 6:10). One needed to be born again to enter His Kingdom (John 3:3). Seeking His kingdom first will put all things into a proper perspective concerning God's program, from creation, that is from the first Adam, to the last Adam and into the eternal state. Christ is the last Adam and He will reign in His covenanted kingdom as the covenanted King with all the redeemed, from the first Adam to the last person saved in the great tribulation.⁴⁹ This is not the church in any sense although the church will reign with Him. The church is not the covenanted kingdom in any sense. George Peters addresses this exact problem many times in his monumental work, *The Theocratic Kingdom*.

> The Church is not like the Kingdom of God once established, *lacking the Theocratic arrangement once instituted*.... The Church is not like

---

⁴⁷ It must be kept in mind that all biblical prophecy about the Messiah will never contradict the biblical covenants, but will arise and flow from them. He will never break any of these unconditional covenants for He cannot violate His word even to the slightest tittle or minutia.

⁴⁸ ζητέω ... try to find something *seek, look for* in order to find ... *desire to possess* τὶ *something*...Mt 6:33; Lk 12:31. William Arndt, Frederick W. Danker, and Walter Bauer, *A Greek-English Lexicon of the New Testament and Other Early Christian Literature* (Chicago: University of Chicago Press, 2000), 428.

⁴⁹ They are all saved eternally by means of or through His covenanted blood i.e. the new covenant which He is mediating at the present time in the heavenly or true tabernacle.

the Kingdom once established *overthrown and promised a restoration*.... The Church is not the Kingdom, otherwise the disciples were *ignorant* of what they preached... that the Church is the promised Kingdom is opposed *by the covenants* ... the preaching of the Kingdom as nigh and then its *postponement* is against making the Church a Kingdom... The simple fact is, that if we once take the covenanted promises in their plain sense, and view the testimony of Scripture sustaining such a sense, it is *utterly impossible* to convert the Church into the promised Kingdom without a *violation* of propriety and unity of Divine Purpose.[50]

When Christ returns to the earth, He will then take His *glorious* throne which was promised to David in the Davidic covenant (2 Sam. 7:12-16). It must be noted here that the church does not have any covenant made with it. The church does or should celebrate the new covenant especially the blood of redemption during communion. But, the church does not have a covenanted throne or a king as promised in the Davidic covenant. The church is not a taste of His coming kingdom in any sense. "But when the Son of Man comes in His glory, and all the angels with Him, then He will sit on His glorious throne" (2 Sam. 7:12-16; Mat. 25:31). Only when He returns then He will take the covenanted throne on the earth. There is no Davidic throne in heaven as this thought or premise is nowhere presented in Scripture except by some men's machinations.

The throne and kingdom of David will be forever. "And your house and your kingdom shall endure before Me forever; your throne shall be established forever" (2 Sam. 7:16). God swore by His holiness that He will fulfill every word in the Davidic covenant. There is no other such oath in the Text. God certainly did not have to do this, but this fully confirms that He unquestionably intends to carry out His every word in the covenants, and unconditionally and literally word for Word.

"I have found David My servant; With My holy oil I have anointed him, [21] with whom My hand will be established; My arm also will

---

[50] George N. H. Peters, *The Theocratic Kingdom*, 3 vols. (Grand Rapids: Kregel Publications, 1988), 1:612.

> strengthen him" (Ps. 89:20-21); "So I will establish his descendants forever, And his throne as the days of heaven. ³⁰ If his sons forsake My law, and do not walk in My judgments, ³¹ If they violate My statutes, and do not keep My commandments, ³² Then I will visit their transgression with the rod, And their iniquity with stripes. ³³But I will not break off My lovingkindness from him, Nor deal falsely in My faithfulness. ³⁴ My covenant I will not violate, nor will I alter the utterance of My lips. ³⁵ <u>Once I have sworn by My holiness; I will not lie to David.</u> ³⁶His descendants shall endure forever, And his throne as the sun before Me. ³⁷ "It shall be established forever like the moon, And the witness in the sky is faithful." Selah. (Ps. 89:30-37 NAS)

This eternal, unconditional covenant is inviolable. It does not depend on David, his sons, or anyone. It will be established forever as the sun, moon, and stars. There is a massive amount of details related to the Person of the Jewish Messiah concerning His covenanted position as King of Israel. This concerns especially His essential genealogy as the covenanted Heir to the covenanted Davidic throne and kingdom. This is why Messiah's genealogy is so critical (Mat. 1:1-17), as He is by biblically covenanted decree the only *par excellence* Davidic Jewish Heir Apparent to the Jewish throne and kingdom.

He will reign 1,000 years until He has put down all rule and authority. Then He will transfer His kingdom to the eternal state. "Then *comes* the end, when He delivers up the kingdom to the God and Father, when He has abolished all rule and all authority and power. For He must reign until He has put all His enemies under His feet" (1 Cor. 15:24-25). The first Adam failed. The last Adam reigns supreme as the perfect God-man, Jesus Christ the King of kings and Lord of lords.

Conclusion

Based on the biblical covenants, especially the Davidic, the Davidic throne and kingdom by covenanted and antitypical design, cannot be changed even minutely without vitiating the original intent of His archetypal plan, purpose, and goal. If this were possible, which it is not, then perhaps God is not able to carry out His program designed around the Jewish nation Israel, or He has deceived Israel and all the other the nations. Or has He completely abandoned His oath-bound covenants sealed with His blood and even swore by His own Person and holiness to carry out?

How utterly inconceivable are the arrogance and audacity of those who do not just simply accept the promises God has declared and proven to be true by His Word. It would seem many more teachers and students of the Word would be more reticent about making bold assertions in which they are so confident, if they relied more on the inerrant words of Scripture and details rather than on any errant theological system.

To replace Israel in any way with any other people, nation, or theology is to violate the truths and promises of all the biblical covenants and prophecies in the Word of God. The church is not defined or described by any of the biblical covenants or prophecies save one and that given by Christ Himself: "And I also say to you that you are Peter, and upon this rock I will build My church; and the gates of Hades shall not overpower it" (Mat 16:18). Only Christ, the last Adam can build His church, His body, and that is what He is doing today. Israel was never designated as His body. He is building His church during this dispensation by His own words.

Israel is defined by His eternal and unconditional covenants with Abraham, Isaac, Jacob, and David. And Israel is created and designed exclusively by and for the great Designer. "But now, thus says the LORD, your Creator, O Jacob, And He who formed you, O Israel, Do not fear, for I have redeemed you; I have called you by name; you are Mine!" (Is. 43:1); "I am the LORD, your Holy One, the Creator of Israel, your King" (Is. 43:15). Pertaining to the Jewish people, even a basic understanding of Judaism is the realization that all the biblical covenants are primarily with Israel. He is coming back for He is the last Adam, the King of Israel. "And so the chief priests of the Jews were saying to Pilate, do not write, The King of the Jews; but that He said, I am King of the Jews" (John 19:21).

God's heavenly eternal throne is established in righteousness, justice, and His loving kindness. "Righteousness and justice are the foundation of Thy throne; Lovingkindness and truth go before Thee" (Ps. 89:14). "Clouds and thick darkness surround Him; righteousness and justice are the foundation of His throne" (Ps. 97:2). God by covenant design established the Davidic throne on earth to bring about justice and righteousness. "Blessed be the LORD your God who delighted in you, setting you on His throne as king for the LORD your God; because your God loved Israel establishing them forever, therefore He made you king over them, to do justice and righteousness" (2 Chr. 9:8). Justice, righteousness, and loving kindness were to permeate the Davidic throne through all the earth.

One day the last Adam, the Creator and Savior of the world will return to claim the David throne of justice and righteousness on earth over Israel in Jerusalem. "There will be no end to the increase of *His* government or of peace, on the throne of David and over his kingdom, to establish it and to uphold it with justice and righteousness from then on and forevermore. The zeal of the LORD of hosts will accomplish this" (Is. 9:7). "A throne will even be established in lovingkindness, and a judge will sit on it in faithfulness in the tent of David; moreover, he will seek justice and be prompt in righteousness" (Is. 16:5). This is not happening in any sense today. The church is not the kingdom nor is Christ building His kingdom or any kingdom. He is building His church, His body, His bride to be and reign with Him forever.

The last Adam is Creator, Savior, High Priest, King of Israel, King of Kings, Lord of Lords and much more. "Then a cloud formed, overshadowing them and a voice came out of the cloud, this is My beloved Son, listen to Him!" (Mar. 9:7). One must make a decision concerning the Son, which is, who is He? "Jesus said to him, I am the way, and the truth, and the life; no one comes to the Father, but through Me" (John14:6). Jesus eliminates all paths to the Father but by one way. The last Adam is the one and only way to the Father. There is nothing grander in this life than to believe and study the Person and greatness of the last Adam.

Appendix A

In the beginning

"**In the beginning** God created the heavens and the earth"[1]

בְּרֵאשִׁית בָּרָא אֱלֹהִים אֵת הַשָּׁמַיִם וְאֵת הָאָרֶץ

There has been much debate over the opening words of Genesis 1:1 especially the terms בְּרֵאשִׁית 'in the beginning' and בָּרָא אֱלֹהִים 'God created.' The issues concerning בְּרֵאשִׁית 'in the beginning' include:

1. a definitive absolute beginning and precise order of all His creation (Gen. 1:1-2:3)
2. a somewhat relative beginning of creation
3. a possible recreation of preexisting material or matter.[2]

What is addressed here is the term בְּרֵאשִׁית particularly its construction and use. Is the Text referring to an absolute beginning of all creation i.e. time, space, matter, man, angels, and much more, or something relative as 'when God began to create,' 'in the beginning when God created,' or even a recreation? There are other possibilities as various translations and commentators try to prove.

What needs to be determined is the basic lexical meaning of בְּרֵאשִׁית and the contextual use for this expression. The true meaning of any word and use will always include context, context, and then context.

Lexical meanings of רֵאשִׁית and the preposition בְּ

---

[1] The debate concerns בְּרֵאשִׁית בָּרָא אֱלֹהִים אֵת הַשָּׁמַיִם וְאֵת הָאָרֶץ 'in the beginning.' A plain and simple reading of Scripture teaches this is the absolute creation account from an absolute beginning.

[2] There are actually several theories of creation but not all are presented here.

BDB רֵאשִׁית ... beginning, chief... Gn 1:1 *in the beginning when god created* (> abs. *in the beginning God created*)[3]

HALOT רֵאשִׁית—1. what comes first, beginning: —a. בְּרֵאשִׁית in (at) the beginning Gn 1₁...
2. beginning, starting point: ...3. the first and best...4. in the context of ritual, first-fruit, choicest portion as a tithe...[4]

Langenscheidt רֵאשִׁית ... beginning, commencement, origin, former state, the first, the best, and firstling.[5]

בְּ ... (preposition) in ... before tone-syllables in certain cases ... **5.** applied to *time*, as Genesis 1:1 בְּרֵאשִׁית *in* the beginning; [6]

Brown Driver Briggs (BDB) gives the basic meaning of רֵאשִׁית beginning, chief, Gen. 1:1 *in the beginning when God created* rendering a relative beginning using a dependent clause (protasis). While in parentheses BDB renders the meaning (> abs. *in the beginning God created*) in the absolute state[7] with the inseparable preposition בְּ as בְּרֵאשִׁית 'in the beginning God created' rendering a main and independent clause. As an independent clause, this was the absolute beginning of all

---

[3] Francis Brown, Samuel Rolles Driver, and Charles Augustus Briggs, *Enhanced Brown-Driver-Briggs Hebrew and English Lexicon* (Oxford: Clarendon Press, 1977), 912.
[4] "רֵאשׁוֹת," *HALOT*, 3:1169-1170.
[5] *Langenscheidt Pocket Dictionary*, p. 310.
[6] Francis Brown, Samuel Rolles Driver, and Charles Augustus Briggs, <u>Enhanced Brown-Driver-Briggs Hebrew and English Lexicon</u> (Oxford: Clarendon Press, 1977), 88.
[7] In Hebrew two nouns or more in sequence may form a construct such as two words 'man house'. In Hebrew reading right to left, this would mean 'a man's house.' The word house would be called the construct and the word for man would be called the absolute. Only the absolute in Hebrew may be articulated i.e. have the article 'the'.

creation and origin of all created things and beings. This would also mean Gen. 1:1 is an independent clause not a protasis[8] with a later apodosis.

It is important to note that רֵאשִׁית is in the absolute state, and only the absolute can be articulated. Because most all translations include the article 'in *the* beginning,' various writers, commentators indicate this word might be considered a construct i.e. 'the beginning of creation, the beginning of the creation or something similar.'

The following are all the uses of בְּרֵאשִׁית in the entire Text, and it must be noted that all uses are in the construct except Genesis 1:1. This is why this is so crucial to understand the usage in Genesis 1:1.

בְּרֵאשִׁית is used five times in the Text

1. Genesis 1:1 **In the beginning** (*absolute*) God created the heavens and the earth.

   בְּרֵאשִׁית בָּרָא אֱלֹהִים אֵת הַשָּׁמַיִם וְאֵת הָאָרֶץ׃

2. Jeremiah 26:1 **In the beginning of the reign of Jehoiakim** (*construct*) the son of Josiah, king of Judah, this word came from the LORD, saying…

   בְּרֵאשִׁית מַמְלְכוּת יְהוֹיָקִים בֶּן־יֹאשִׁיָּהוּ מֶלֶךְ יְהוּדָה הָיָה הַדָּבָר הַזֶּה מֵאֵת יְהוָה לֵאמֹר׃

3. Jeremiah 27:1 **In the beginning of the reign of Zedekiah** (*construct*) the son of Josiah, king of Judah, this word came to Jeremiah from the LORD, saying…

   בְּרֵאשִׁית מַמְלֶכֶת יְהוֹיָקִם בֶּן־יֹאושִׁיָּהוּ מֶלֶךְ יְהוּדָה הָיָה הַדָּבָר הַזֶּה אֶל־יִרְמְיָה מֵאֵת יְהוָה לֵאמֹר׃

---

[8] Protasis – an if, when or other dependent clause and then the apodosis i.e. the main clause. Genesis 1:1 is simply a main clause.

4. Jeremiah 28:1 Now it came about in the same year, (*construct*) **in the beginning of the reign of Zedekiah** king of Judah…

וַיְהִי בַּשָּׁנָה הַהִיא **בְּרֵאשִׁית מַמְלֶכֶת צִדְקִיָּה מֶלֶךְ־יְהוּדָה**

5. Jeremiah 49:34 That which came as the word of the LORD to Jeremiah the prophet concerning Elam, **at the beginning of the reign of Zedekiah** (*construct*) king of Judah, saying…

אֲשֶׁר הָיָה דְבַר־יְהוָה אֶל־יִרְמְיָהוּ הַנָּבִיא אֶל־עֵילָם **בְּרֵאשִׁית מַלְכוּת צִדְקִיָּה** מֶלֶךְ־יְהוּדָה לֵאמֹר׃

The primary use of **בְּרֵאשִׁית** is in the construct state as shown above specifically in Jer. 26:1; 27:1; 28:1; and 49:34. But in Gen. 1:1 it is not used as a construct in any sense; it is an absolute as by grammatical definition in that context. The other four uses have similar contexts as constructs but Gen. 1:1 is completely different and should be understood in time or more adverbially.

Genesis 1:1 **בְּרֵאשִׁית** is not a construct as some translators or commentators may try to prove. A construct in Hebrew are simply nouns in sequence[9] which usually make a construct chain (it may not under certain conditions) and the last noun is called the absolute. It must be noted that the construct cannot be articulated in Hebrew, only the last noun or absolute may be articulated for the construct chain.[10]

---

[9] This would be a 'noun noun' or many more nouns. But the chain from right to left in Hebrew would appear 'construct absolute' or with many nouns 'construct construct, etc absolute'. There is only one absolute and only that can be articulated.

[10] The normal word meaning is always given in the absolute and again, only the absolute can be articulated.

The absolute does not need to be articulated

But in Hebrew even the absolute does not need to be articulated in the construct chain to have articulation for the construct.[11] Note the following examples and there are others.

Psalm 111:10 The fear of the LORD is **the** beginning of wisdom; a good understanding have all those who do *His commandments*; His praise endures forever.

רֵאשִׁ֤ית חָכְמָ֨ה ׀ יִרְאַ֬ת יְהוָ֗ה שֵׂ֣כֶל ט֖וֹב לְכָל־עֹשֵׂיהֶ֑ם תְּ֝הִלָּת֗וֹ עֹמֶ֥דֶת לָעַֽד׃

Genesis 49:3 "Reuben, you are my first-born; My might and **the** beginning of my strength, Preeminent in dignity and preeminent in power.

רְאוּבֵן֙ בְּכֹ֣רִי אַ֔תָּה כֹּחִ֖י **וְרֵאשִׁ֣ית אוֹנִ֑י** יֶ֥תֶר שְׂאֵ֖ת וְיֶ֥תֶר עָֽז׃

Numbers 24:20 And he looked at Amalek and took up his discourse and said, "Amalek was **the** first of the nations, But his end *shall be* destruction."

וַיַּ֣רְא אֶת־עֲמָלֵ֔ק וַיִּשָּׂ֥א מְשָׁל֖וֹ וַיֹּאמַ֑ר **רֵאשִׁ֤ית גּוֹיִם֙** עֲמָלֵ֔ק וְאַחֲרִית֖וֹ עֲדֵ֥י אֹבֵֽד׃

A noun with a preposition may be articulated

Even a noun with a preposition may be articulated when referring to time and other aspects while not being articulated in Hebrew itself. The following examples prove such a point.

---

[11] This does not mean 'in the beginning of the creation or a creation' as if this were a construct. There are those who believe בְּרֵאשִׁית should be considered a construct because of the use of articulation being used in Gen. 1:1 'in the beginning of a/the creation.' But the construct does not need the absolute to be articulated to have articulation.

2 Chronicles 25:27 And from the time that Amaziah turned away from following the LORD they conspired against him in Jerusalem, and he fled to Lachish; but they sent after him to Lachish and killed him there.

וּמֵ**עֵת** אֲשֶׁר־סָר אֲמַצְיָהוּ מֵאַחֲרֵי יְהוָה וַיִּקְשְׁרוּ עָלָיו קֶשֶׁר בִּירוּשָׁלַם וַיָּנָס לָכִישָׁה וַיִּשְׁלְחוּ אַחֲרָיו לָכִישָׁה וַיְמִיתֻהוּ שָׁם:

2 Chronicles 25:27 καὶ ἐν τῷ καιρῷ ᾧ ἀπέστη Αμασιας ἀπὸ κυρίου καὶ ἐπέθεντο αὐτῷ ἐπίθεσιν καὶ ἔφυγεν ἀπὸ Ιερουσαλημ εἰς Λαχις καὶ ἀπέστειλαν κατόπισθεν αὐτοῦ εἰς Λαχις καὶ ἐθανάτωσαν αὐτὸν ἐκεῖ (Note: *even the LXX recognizes this from the Hebrew*)

Isaiah 46:10 Declaring **the end from the beginning**[12] and from ancient times things which have not been done, Saying, 'My purpose will be established, And I will accomplish all My good pleasure

מַגִּיד מֵ**רֵאשִׁית אַחֲרִית** וּמִקֶּדֶם אֲשֶׁר לֹא־נַעֲשׂוּ אֹמֵר עֲצָתִי תָקוּם וְכָל־חֶפְצִי אֶעֱשֶׂה:

Isaiah 48:16 "Come near to Me, listen to this: **From the first** I have not spoken in secret, **From the time** it took place, I was there. And now the Lord God has sent Me, and His Spirit."

קִרְבוּ אֵלַי שִׁמְעוּ־זֹאת לֹא מֵ**רֹאשׁ** בַּסֵּתֶר דִּבַּרְתִּי מֵ**עֵת** הֱיוֹתָהּ שָׁם אָנִי וְעַתָּה אֲדֹנָי יְהוִה שְׁלָחַנִי וְרוּחוֹ:

---

[12] It is important to note Isaiah 46:10 where the construction is identical with Gen. 1:1 i.e. a preposition and a noun having no article/s with the noun in the absolute state yet translated with articulation. Note also this is a back to back construction of that being discussed i.e. a preposition with a noun used adverbially.

פ

Note Is. 46:10 'the end from the beginning' מֵרֵאשִׁית אַחֲרִית even the LXX from Gen. 1:1 has the same basic construction i.e. a preposition without the article בְּרֵאשִׁית. LXX ἐν ἀρχῇ[13] ἐποίησεν ὁ θεὸς τὸν οὐρανὸν καὶ τὴν γῆν. In principio creavit Deus caelum et terram[14] John 1:1 follows this same construction. "**In the beginning** was the Word, and the Word was with God, and the Word was God" Ἐν ἀρχῇ ἦν ὁ λόγος, καὶ ὁ λόγος ἦν πρὸς τὸν θεόν, καὶ θεὸς ἦν ὁ λόγος. Robertson makes this comment, "**In the beginning** (ἐν ἀρχῃ [*en archēi*]). Ἀρχη [*Archē*] is definite, though anarthrous like our at home, in town, and the similar Hebrew *be reshith* [*bərē'šît*; בְּרֵאשִׁית] in Gen. 1:1."[15] This is simply normal construction using the normal use of the biblical languages.

Context

The immediate context is always going to be the major determinant for translating when there are various meanings or nuances for any word. *"In the beginning God created the heaven and the earth."*—Heaven and earth have not existed from all eternity, but had a beginning; nor did they arise by emanation from an absolute substance, but were created by God. This sentence, which stands at the head of the records of revelation, is not a mere heading, nor a summary of the history of the creation, but a declaration of the primeval act of God, by

---

[13] [UBS] ἀρχή, ῆς f beginning, first … origin, first cause; ruling power, authority, ruler (whether earthly or spiritual); what is elementary, elementary principle … [Fri] ἀρχή, ῆς, ἡ strictly *primacy*;… ἀπ ἀρχῆς, ἐξ ἀρχῆς *from the first, originally* (JN 6.64; 15.27); ἐν ἀρχῇ, κατ ἀρχάς *in the beginning, at the first* (JN 1.1; HE 1.10)…[LS] ἀρχή, ἡ, (ἄρχω) *a beginning, origin, first cause*.
[14] *Biblia Sacra Vulgata: Iuxta Vulgatem Versionem*, electronic edition of the 3rd edition. (Stuttgart: Deutsche Bibelgesellschaft, 1969), Ge 1:1.
[15] A.T. Robertson, *Word Pictures in the New Testament* (Nashville, TN: Broadman Press, 1933), Jn 1:1.

which the universe was called into being. That this verse is not a heading merely, is evident from the fact that the following account of the course of the creation commences with וְ (*and*), which connects the different acts of creation with the fact expressed in v. 1, as the primary foundation upon which they rest. בְּרֵאשִׁית (in the beginning) is used absolutely, like ἐν ἀρχῇ in John 1:1, and מֵרֵאשִׁית in Isa. 46:10." [16]

Conclusion

The normal use for בְּרֵאשִׁית is a genitive construct with articulation (Jer. 26:1; 27:1; 28:1; 49:34). However, Genesis 1:1 is clearly an absolute with the inseparable preposition בְּ. The parsing for בְּרֵאשִׁית is the inseparable preposition בְּ with רֵאשִׁית noun common feminine singular absolute. The articulation if used is simply a normal use of the language where certain expressions perhaps adverbial expressions do not necessarily need the article. Certain words or terms as רֵאשִׁית beginning 'when used in adverbial expressions occur almost invariably without the article, and that in the absolute state' [17]

As has been shown Isaiah 46:10 makes it obvious that רֵאשִׁית with the inseparable preposition מֵ does not need the article 'from the beginning' מֵרֵאשִׁית. The creation referred to in context of Gen. 1:1ff and in all these verses had an absolute beginning by an absolutely Sovereign Creator. There is no ambiguity in any of these verses or any of the Text revealing any kind of gap or gap theory. There is nothing relative concerning creation or a recreation as such by the Son of God. If Jesus as Creator judged His creation prior to Gen. 1:1 or just after because of the sin/s of angels or man, etc. there is absolutely no proof in all the Text for any such teaching. One would have to prove the Son of God created everything and

---

[16] Carl Friedrich Keil and Franz Delitzsch, *Commentary on the Old Testament*, vol. 1 (Peabody, MA: Hendrickson, 1996), 28.
[17] W.W. Fields, *Unformed and Unfilled, A Critique of the Gap Theory*, (Collinsville, Il: Burgener Enterprises, 1992), p. 153.

then destroyed or judged it, and then He refashioned it.

Scripture reveals one Creator and one creation. There is absolutely no such teaching of multiple creations, a recreation, or any prior creation before Genesis 1:1, John 1:1-3; Col. 1:16, Heb. 11:3, and many other related verses in the Text.

But time wise as in origin or 'originally' this might best be translated 'Originally God created' never 'when God began to create.' The use and construction of בְּרֵאשִׁית will not support any concept or proof of a recreation. Originally when God began to recreate the creation? The expression בְּרֵאשִׁית בָּרָא [18]אֱלֹהִים in context will not support any of this. This could also be translated 'in origin' asserting the truly absolute beginning or a starting point[19] of God's creation.

---

[18] Note the preposition בְּ in context makes this expression with the absolute רֵאשִׁית 'applied to time' stressing an adverbial use.

[19] רֵשִׁית Dt 11$_{13}$: sf. רֵאשִׁיתְךָ, רֵאשִׁיתוֹ: רֵאשִׁית: — 1. what is first, **beginning** Is 46$_{10}$; — 2. **beginning, starting-point**: time Gn 1$_1$; (pg 330)

Appendix B

Formless and void

ṭōhû wāḇōhû תֹ֙הוּ֙ וָבֹ֔הוּ

"And the earth was **formless and void**, and darkness was over the surface of the deep; and the Spirit of God was moving over the surface of the waters" (Gen. 1:2).

Gen. 1:2 וְהָאָ֗רֶץ הָיְתָ֥ה **תֹ֙הוּ֙ וָבֹ֔הוּ** וְחֹ֖שֶׁךְ עַל־פְּנֵ֣י תְה֑וֹם וְר֣וּחַ אֱלֹהִ֔ים מְרַחֶ֖פֶת עַל־פְּנֵ֥י הַמָּֽיִם׃

The basic meanings of תֹ֙הוּ֙ וָבֹ֔הוּ are as follows from the *Enhanced Brown-Driver-Briggs Hebrew and English Lexicon*.

> תֹּ֫הוּ *ṭōhû* ... n.m. ... formlessness, confusion, unreality, emptiness (primary meaning difficult to seize; (old versions) usually κενόν, οὐδέν, μάταιον, *inane, vacuum, vanum*; ...—**1. formlessness, of primaeval earth Gn 1:2** ...of land reduced to primaeval chaos Je 4:23 (both ... וָבֹ֔הוּ *and voidness*), Is 34:11 קו־ת׳ (אבני בהו), 45:18 קרית־ת׳ ;24:10 (לשבת יצרה) לא ת׳ בראה *city of chaos* (of ruined city); = *nothingness, empty space*,.[1]

> בֹּ֫הוּ *bōhû* ... n. m. **emptiness** ... always with תֹּ֫הוּ *quod vide* תֹּ֫הוּ וָבֹ֫הוּ **Gn 1:2 of primæval earth;** Je 4:23 of earth under judgment of ׳;w קו־תֹהוּ וְאַבְנֵי בֹהוּ Is 34:11, *the line of wasteness and the stones of emptiness,* i.e. plummets, employed,

---

[1] Francis Brown, Samuel Rolles Driver, and Charles Augustus Briggs, *Enhanced Brown-Driver-Briggs Hebrew and English Lexicon* (Oxford: Clarendon Press, 1977), 1062. ⅏ Greek version of the LXX.

not as usual for building, but for destroying walls;[2]

BDB notes that the basic meaning/s may be difficult but the context is always going to be the key issue and not just a meaning independent of context. The primary lexical definitions for these words *tōhû wābōhû* תֹהוּ וָבֹהוּ are simply formless and void (empty or meaningless). There is one other verse in the Text (Jer. 4:23) which literally uses the words together *tōhû wābōhû* תֹהוּ וָבֹהוּ identically as in Gen. 1:2. This is very informative and very significant.

"I looked on the earth, and behold, *it was* **formless and void**; and to the heavens, and they had no light" (Jer. 4:23).

Jer. 4:23 רָאִ֙יתִי֙ אֶת־הָאָ֔רֶץ וְהִנֵּה־תֹ֖הוּ וָבֹ֑הוּ וְאֶל־הַשָּׁמַ֖יִם וְאֵ֥ין אוֹרָֽם׃

As the context of Genesis 1:2 is the creation of the heavens and the earth, the context of Jeremiah 4:23 is a *future* judgment.

> "For My people are foolish, they know Me not; They are stupid children, and they have no understanding. They are shrewd to do evil, But to do good they do not know. [23] I looked on the earth, and behold, *it was* **formless and void**; and to the heavens, and they had no light. [24] I looked on the mountains, and behold, they were quaking, and all the hills moved to and fro. [25] I looked, and behold, there was no man, and all the birds of the heavens had fled. [26] I looked, and behold, the fruitful land was a wilderness, And

---

[2] Francis Brown, Samuel Rolles Driver, and Charles Augustus Briggs, *Enhanced Brown-Driver-Briggs Hebrew and English Lexicon* (Oxford: Clarendon Press, 1977), 96.

all its cities were pulled down Before the LORD, before His fierce anger. ²⁷ For thus says the LORD, **the whole land shall be a desolation**, yet I will not execute a complete destruction" (Jer. 4:22-27).

The primary meaning/s for any word is always context, context, and then context. Note the context of Jeremiah 4:23 which is referring to a *future* destruction. The words *tōhû wābōhû* are not referring to something already judged and *never* refer to something already judged in any sense. Note well verse 4:27, "The whole land shall be a desolation, yet I will not execute a **complete destruction**" (Jer. 4:22-27). There is no proof that these words *tōhû wābōhû* refer to any past destruction or any complete destruction as some have tried to eisegete into the meaning of the Text especially Genesis 1:2.

The words in Jeremiah are referring to something which is uninhabitable or empty.³ The main idea in Jer. 4:22-27 is referring more to a place unfit to live for any creature and perhaps void of life 'creatures' in every sense.

Other uses of *tōhû* in context hold similar meanings

Deuteronomy 32:10 "He found him in a desert land, and in the howling **waste** of a wilderness; He encircled him, He cared for him, He guarded him as the pupil of His eye."

Deuteronomy 32:10 יִמְצָאֵ֙הוּ֙ בְּאֶ֣רֶץ מִדְבָּ֔ר **וּבְתֹ֖הוּ** יְלֵ֣ל יְשִׁמֹ֑ן
יְסֹבְבֶ֙נְהוּ֙ יְב֣וֹנְנֵ֔הוּ יִצְּרֶ֖נְהוּ כְּאִישׁ֥וֹן עֵינֽוֹ׃

1 Samuel 12:21 "And you must not turn aside, for *then you would go* after **futile things** which cannot profit or deliver, because they are **futile**."

1 Samuel 12:21 וְלֹ֖א תָּס֑וּרוּ כִּ֣י ׀ אַחֲרֵ֣י **הַתֹּ֗הוּ** אֲשֶׁ֧ר לֹֽא־יוֹעִ֛ילוּ וְלֹ֥א
יַצִּ֖ילוּ כִּי־**תֹ֥הוּ** הֵֽמָּה׃

---

³ The words void or something futile as in vain as confusion.

Job 6:18 "The paths of their course wind along, They go up into **nothing** and perish."

Job 6:18 יְלָ֥פְתוּ אָרְח֣וֹת דַּרְכָּ֑ם יַעֲל֖וּ בַתֹּ֣הוּ וְיֹאבֵֽדוּ׃

Job 12:24 "He deprives of intelligence the chiefs of the earth's people, and makes them wander in a pathless **waste**."

Job 12:24 מֵסִ֗יר לֵ֭ב רָאשֵׁ֣י עַם־הָאָ֑רֶץ וַ֝יַּתְעֵ֗ם בְּתֹ֣הוּ לֹא־דָֽרֶךְ׃

Job 26:7 "He stretches out the north over empty space, and hangs the earth on **nothing**."

Job 26:7 נֹטֶ֣ה צָפ֣וֹן עַל־תֹּ֑הוּ תֹּ֥לֶה אֶ֝֗רֶץ עַל־בְּלִי־מָֽה׃

Psalm 107:40 "He pours contempt upon princes, and makes them wander in a pathless **waste**."

Psalm 107:40 שֹׁפֵ֣ךְ בּ֭וּז עַל־נְדִיבִ֑ים וַ֝יַּתְעֵ֗ם בְּתֹ֣הוּ לֹא־דָֽרֶךְ׃

Isaiah 29:21 "Who cause a person to be indicted by a word, And ensnare him who adjudicates at the gate, And defraud the one in the right with **meaningless** arguments."

Isaiah 29:21 מַחֲטִיאֵ֤י אָדָם֙ בְּדָבָ֔ר וְלַמּוֹכִ֥יחַ בַּשַּׁ֖עַר יְקֹשׁ֑וּן וַיַּטּ֥וּ בַתֹּ֖הוּ צַדִּֽיק׃ ס

Isaiah 34:11 uses both words *tōhû wābōhû* **תֹּ֥הוּ וָבֹ֖הוּ** yet with similar meanings. They are so similar that these words are sometimes referred to as a hendiadys.[4]

Isaiah 34:11 "But pelican and hedgehog shall possess it, And

---

[4]hendiadys...noun the expression of a single idea by two words connected with 'and', e.g. *nice and warm*, when one could be used to modify the other, as in *nicely warm*.—ORIGIN 16th century: via medieval Latin from Greek *hen dia duoin* 'one thing by two'. Catherine Soanes and Angus Stevenson, eds., <u>Concise Oxford English Dictionary</u> (Oxford: Oxford University Press, 2004).

owl and raven shall dwell in it; And He shall stretch over it the line of **desolation** And the plumb line of **emptiness**."

Isaiah 34:11 וִירֵשׁ֙וּהָ֙ קָאַ֣ת וְקִפּ֔וֹד וְיַנְשׁ֥וֹף וְעֹרֵ֖ב יִשְׁכְּנוּ־בָ֑הּ וְנָטָ֥ה עָלֶ֛יהָ

קַו־**תֹ֖הוּ** וְאַבְנֵי־בֹֽהוּ׃

Isaiah 40:17 "All the nations are as nothing before Him, They are regarded by Him as less than nothing and **meaningless**."

Isaiah 40:17 כָּל־הַגּוֹיִ֖ם כְּאַ֣יִן נֶגְדּ֑וֹ מֵאֶ֥פֶס וָ**תֹ֖הוּ** נֶחְשְׁבוּ־לֽוֹ׃

Isaiah 40:23 "He *it is* who reduces rulers to nothing, Who makes the judges of the earth **meaningless**."

Isaiah 40:23 הַנּוֹתֵ֥ן רוֹזְנִ֖ים לְאָ֑יִן שֹׁ֥פְטֵי אֶ֖רֶץ כַּ**תֹּ֥הוּ** עָשָֽׂה׃

Isaiah 41:29 "Behold, all of them are false; their works are worthless, Their molten images are wind and **emptiness**."

Isaiah 41:29 הֵ֣ן כֻּלָּ֔ם אָ֖וֶן אֶ֣פֶס מַעֲשֵׂיהֶ֑ם ר֥וּחַ וָ**תֹ֖הוּ** נִסְכֵּיהֶֽם׃ פ

Isaiah 44:9 "Those who fashion a graven image are all of them **futile**, and their precious things are of no profit; even their own witnesses fail to see or know, so that they will be put to shame."

Isaiah 44:9 יֹֽצְרֵי־פֶ֤סֶל כֻּלָּם֙ **תֹּ֔הוּ** וַחֲמוּדֵיהֶ֖ם בַּל־יוֹעִ֑ילוּ וְעֵדֵיהֶ֣ם הֵ֗מָּה

בַּל־יִרְא֛וּ וּבַל־יֵדְע֖וּ לְמַ֥עַן יֵבֹֽשׁוּ׃

Isaiah 45:19 "I have not spoken in secret, In some dark land; I did not say to the offspring of Jacob, 'Seek Me in a **waste place**'; I, the LORD, speak righteousness Declaring things that are upright."

Isaiah 45:19 לֹ֧א בַסֵּ֣תֶר דִּבַּ֗רְתִּי בִּמְק֛וֹם אֶ֥רֶץ חֹ֖שֶׁךְ לֹ֣א אָמַ֗רְתִּי לְזֶ֣רַע

יַעֲקֹ֔ב **תֹּ֖הוּ** בַקְּשׁ֑וּנִי אֲנִ֤י יְהוָה֙ דֹּבֵ֣ר צֶ֔דֶק מַגִּ֖יד מֵישָׁרִֽים׃

Isaiah 49:4 "But I said, I have toiled in vain, I have spent My strength for **nothing** and vanity; Yet surely the justice *due* to Me is with the LORD, And My reward with My God."

Isaiah 49:4 וַאֲנִ֤י אָמַ֙רְתִּי֙ לְרִ֣יק יָגַ֔עְתִּי לְתֹ֥הוּ וְהֶ֖בֶל כֹּחִ֣י כִלֵּ֑יתִי אָכֵן֙ מִשְׁפָּטִ֣י אֶת־יְהוָ֔ה וּפְעֻלָּתִ֖י אֶת־אֱלֹהָֽי׃

Isaiah 59:4 "No one sues righteously and no one pleads honestly. They trust in **confusion**, and speak lies; they conceive mischief, and bring forth iniquity."

Isaiah 59:4 אֵין־קֹרֵ֣א בְצֶ֔דֶק וְאֵ֥ין נִשְׁפָּ֖ט בֶּאֱמוּנָ֑ה בָּט֣וֹחַ עַל־תֹּ֗הוּ וְדַבֶּר־שָׁ֔וְא הָר֥וֹ עָמָ֖ל וְהוֹלֵ֥יד אָֽוֶן׃

The next verse is very significant as to the meaning of *tōhû*.

Isaiah 45:18 "For thus says the LORD, who created the heavens (He is the God who formed the earth and made it, He established it and did not create it a **waste place**, *But* formed it to be inhabited), I am the LORD, and there is none else."

Isaiah 45:18 כִּ֣י כֹ֣ה אָֽמַר־יְ֠הוָה בּוֹרֵ֨א הַשָּׁמַ֜יִם ה֣וּא הָאֱלֹהִ֗ים יֹצֵ֨ר הָאָ֤רֶץ וְעֹשָׂהּ֙ ה֣וּא כֽוֹנְנָ֔הּ לֹא־תֹ֥הוּ בְרָאָ֖הּ לָשֶׁ֣בֶת יְצָרָ֑הּ אֲנִ֥י יְהוָ֖ה וְאֵ֥ין עֽוֹד׃

One has to note the construction in verse 45:18 (please see Appendix C for more information). The Scripture never stated that God created the earth a 'waste place' it just says 'it was in this state.' The negation לֹא in 45:18 is before the word *tōhû* לֹא־תֹ֥הוּ and not before the word 'created.' This is significant as 'not *tōhû*' He created it. God never 'created the earth' to be formless i.e. uninhabitable or to remain in this condition as formless as the Text proves in context. Note a waste place or formless He created it but "formed it to be inhabited" I am the LORD, and there is none else."

The condition of all the creation was flawless in Gen. 1:1 that is absolutely perfect. Every planet could be called *tōhû wābōhû* but only earth was created to be inhabited and not 'a waste place' formless or *tōhû*.

The next verse also presents an unusual meaning for the word.

Isaiah 24:10 The city of **chaos** is broken down; Every house is shut up so that none may enter.

Isaiah 24:10 נִשְׁבְּרָה קִרְיַת־**תֹּהוּ** סֻגַּר כָּל־בַּיִת מִבּוֹא׃

The word chaos in various translations is often used to prove that God could not have produced 'a chaos' i.e. a complete disorder or confusion. Therefore a gap of time is understood after Gen. 1:1 yet prior to Gen. 1:2 which may be defined by some as 'a gap theory'. There are variations to this such as the pre-creation chaos theory.[5] This might be defined as a creation prior to Gen. 1:1 which was subsequently destroyed and then Gen. 1:1 is the creation or recreation which is being revealed. There are even variations with this view.

The problem is rather simple to solve without any gap at all. What is the biblical meaning of the word 'chaos?' The ancients would not understand a later word meaning especially from the 20th or 21st centuries. The Greeks or Hellenists had a particular meaning as well as Rome (Latin). A very simple and basic meaning explains much.

While many commentators seem to go to the more modern meaning/s of chaos, very few attempt or give the possibility of an earlier meaning for this word.

> **chaos** ... 1 complete disorder and confusion… the property of a complex system whose behavior is so unpredictable as to appear random, owing to great sensitivity to small changes in conditions…
> 2 the formless matter supposed to have

---

[5] Many more creationists seem to be moving towards this view.

existed before the creation of the universe. — ORIGIN **15th century (denoting a gaping void): via French and Latin from Greek** *khaos* **'vast chasm, void'.**[6]

The second meaning is closer to the truth of what 'chaos' would be to the Greek/Semitic mind. In fact there are translations which reflect this.[7]

Observe the earliest and primary meaning of chaos as 'an empty, immeasurable space' a yawning chasm.' This best reflects the true meaning of this word.[8] Yet this is already acknowledged in BDB.

> תֹּהוּ *tōhû* … n.m. … formlessness, confusion, unreality, emptiness (primary meaning difficult to seize; (old versions) usually κενόν, οὐδέν, μάταιον, *inane, vacuum, vanum;* …—1. *formlessness*, of primaeval earth Gn 1:2 …of land reduced to **primaeval chaos** Je 4:23 (both … וָבֹהוּ *and voidness*), Is 34:11 (קַו־תֹּהוּ (אַבְנֵי בֹהוּ), **24:10** קִרְיַת־תֹּהוּ *city of chaos* (of ruined city); = *nothingness, empty space*, 45:18 (לְשֶׁבֶת יְצָרָהּ לֹא תֹהוּ בְרָאָהּ).[9]

---

[6] Catherine Soanes and Angus Stevenson, eds., *Concise Oxford English Dictionary* (Oxford: Oxford University Press, 2004).
[7] Note Luke 16:26 in the NASB and Douay-Rheims and others.
[8] Note the LXX: **Genesis 1:2** And the earth was **formless and void**, and darkness was over the surface of the deep; and the Spirit of God was moving over the surface of the waters. The simple meaning from the LXX is simply not visible and unformed. LXX ἡ δὲ γῆ ἦν **ἀόρατος καὶ ἀκατασκεύαστος** καὶ σκότος ἐπάνω τῆς ἀβύσσου καὶ πνεῦμα θεοῦ ἐπεφέρετο ἐπάνω τοῦ ὕδατος. **ἀόρατος** adjective normal nominative feminine singular no degree from **ἀόρατος** [LS] **ἀόρατος,** ov, *unseen, not to be seen, invisible,* Plat., etc. II. act. *without sight,* Luc…[LXX Suppl] **ἀοράτως** *invisibly* **ἀκατασκεύαστος** adjective normal nominative feminine singular no degree… [LXX Suppl] **ἀκατασκεύαστος,** -ov; *unformed…* [LEH] … Gn 1,2 *unwrought, unformed, unorganized…*
[9] Francis Brown, Samuel Rolles Driver, and Charles Augustus Briggs,

The basic etymology of the word chaos is so crucial, and it is easily proven the earlier meaning of chaos is very consistent.

> Cha′os (kā′ŏs), *n.* [L. *chaos* chaos (in senses 1 & 2), Gr. χάος, fr. χάινειν (root χα) to yawn, to gape, to open widely. Cf. Chasm.] 1. **An empty, immeasurable space; a yawning chasm. [Archaic] Between us and there is fixed a great** *chaos*. *Luke xvi. 26. (Rhemish Trans.).*
> 2. The confused, unorganized condition or mass of matter before the creation of distinct and orderly forms.
> 3. Any confused or disordered collection or state of things; a confused mixture; confusion; disorder.[10]

Note well what many translators used as basic meaning, yet the true meaning of chaos is a great space or chasm. This can be proven easily from the New Testament Greek.

Luke 16:26 καὶ ἐν πᾶσι τούτοις μεταξὺ ἡμῶν καὶ ὑμῶν **χάσμα** μέγα ἐστήρικται, ὅπως οἱ θέλοντες διαβῆναι ἔνθεν πρὸς ὑμᾶς μὴ δύνωνται, μηδὲ ἐκεῖθεν πρὸς ἡμᾶς διαπερῶσιν.

Luke 16:26 "And besides all this, between us and you there is a **great chasm** fixed, in order that those who wish to come over from here to you may not be able, and *that* none may cross over from there to us." (NASB)

Luke 16:26 "And besides all this, between us and you, there is fixed a **great chaos**: so that they who would pass from hence to

---

Enhanced Brown-Driver-Briggs Hebrew and English Lexicon (Oxford: Clarendon Press, 1977), 1062. ⅏ Greek version of the LXX.
[10]*Webster's Revised Unabridged Dictionary*, s.v. "Chaos," paragraph 36753.

you, cannot, nor from thence come hither." (Douay-Rheims)[11]

The modern meaning of chaos does not equate with any Text or translation which includes 'any confused or disordered collection or state of things; a confused mixture; confusion; disorder.' The only disorder which might be included with the infinitely flawless creation was that it was yet unformed for human habitation.

> "The Greek concept of chaos was an infinitude of empty space. The later Roman concept viewed chaos as "Rudis indigestaque moles" i.e., "A shapeless mass unwrought and unordered." The Roman concept, more than the Greek, seems to approximate the contemporary English conception of the word: "the confused unorganized state of primordial matter before creation and distinct forms." There is little doubt that the Hebrew concept of the earth described as *tohu* and *bohu* would not have matched the Greek concept of chaos, for the word *bara* is used for creation, and it is doubtful that God would have created a nothingness, when, presumably, a nothingness already existed. Furthermore, *the LXX translation did not use the Greek word "chaos" in translating tohu and bohu*! Moreover, no recognized Greek translation has ever done so."[12]

It would be best not to use the word chaos unless the earliest and foremost meaning is given primary and crucial

---

[11] The **Douay–Rheims** is a translation from the Latin Vulgate into English made by members of the English College, Douai, and the New Testament was published in Reims, France, in 1582.
[12] Weston W. Fields, *Unformed and Unfilled* (Illinois: Burgener Enterprises, 1997), p. 125.

etymological consideration.

Conclusion

The primary meaning of *tōhû wābōhû* is simply formless and void and has no association with something which has been judged in any sense. There is also no relation to some chaotic state as a later or perhaps 21st century meaning. There is nothing even associated with evil but just that which the context allows that is 'unformed.'[13] Genesis 1:1 describes a perfect creation with no flaws. The concept of *tōhû wābōhû* in context of Genesis 1:2 is simply that the perfect earth was not yet formed for men's habitation and dominion to rule under their Creator.

> "When I consider Thy heavens, the work of Thy fingers, the moon and the stars, which Thou hast ordained; [4] what is man, that Thou dost take thought of him? and the son of man, that Thou dost care for him? [5] Yet Thou hast made him a little lower than God, And dost crown him with glory and majesty! [6] Thou dost make him to rule over the works of Thy hands; Thou hast put all things under his feet" (Ps. 8:3-6).

All of God's creation was ultimately made to bring glory to the Creator especially from man created in His image. The truth is that God has created, made, formed, etc. the earth for man to dwell and have communion with his Creator until the eternal state. It was created flawless in literal 6 days by the infinitely flawless Creator and it was all very good.

---

[13] וּבֹ֫הוּ *tōhû* ... n.m. ... formlessness,. Francis Brown, Samuel Rolles Driver, and Charles Augustus Briggs, *Enhanced Brown-Driver-Briggs Hebrew and English Lexicon* (Oxford: Clarendon Press, 1977), 1062.

> "And God saw all that He had made, and behold, it was very good. And there was evening and there was morning, the sixth day. Thus the heavens and the earth were completed, and all their hosts. ² And by the seventh day God completed His work which He had done; and He rested on the seventh day from all His work which He had done. ³ Then God blessed the seventh day and sanctified it, because in it He rested from all His work which God had created and made" (Gen 1:31-2:3).

If there were an angelic battle ensuing at the end of the 6th day, nothing would be very good and there would be little or no rest on the 7th day. It is amazing how much superfluous material is read into the literal ex-nihilo creation account of Genesis 1:1-2:4.[14]

---

[14] Please see Appendix E concerning Heb. 11:3.

Appendix C

Isaiah 45:18

Those who hold to any form of a gap theory[1] usually refer to Isaiah 45:18 as a major text for their speculation of creation with 'a gap.' This verse is often used as a major proof text for their meaning of *tōhû* in context of Gen. 1:1-1:2 and Is. 45:18. As this has been somewhat addressed already, there is more which must be taken into consideration.

Genesis 1

In Genesis 1:1 it is very clear God created the heavens and the earth.[2]

"In the beginning God created the heavens and the earth"[3] (Genesis 1:1).

בְּרֵאשִׁית בָּרָא אֱלֹהִים אֵת הַשָּׁמַיִם וְאֵת הָאָרֶץ׃

Most of the disagreements ensue from Gen. 1:2 with the expression 'and the earth was formless and void.'

---

[1] One must realize as has been noted before there are various theories concerning creation especially those who hold to a gap of time. "And by the seventh day God completed His work which He had done; and He rested on the seventh day from all His work which He had done" (Gen. 2:2).

[2] There is absolutely nothing in the context of Genesis 1:1 to 1:2 that proves any kind of judgment, catastrophe, or destruction on the earth to cause what some believe is a 'chaos' or a judged earth resulting in its being formless and void (*tōhû wābōhû*). There was absolutely nothing which caused the earth to be formless and void, it simply was in its originally created state. As has been shown in Appendix A the expression has nothing to do with a judged earth or a judged anything. There is so much read into these verses by commentators that it is impossible to deal with all of them.

[3] The Scripture never stated that God created the earth a 'waste place' it just says 'it was unformed and unfilled.'

"And the earth was **formless and void**, and darkness was over the surface of the deep; and the Spirit of God was moving over the surface of the waters" (Genesis 1:2).

וְהָאָ֗רֶץ הָיְתָ֥ה **תֹ֙הוּ֙ וָבֹ֔הוּ** וְחֹ֖שֶׁךְ עַל־פְּנֵ֣י תְה֑וֹם וְר֣וּחַ אֱלֹהִ֔ים מְרַחֶ֖פֶת עַל־פְּנֵ֥י הַמָּֽיִם׃

From the simple reading of Genesis 1:1 to 1:2 there is absolutely nothing in the context proving any kind of judgment, catastrophe, destruction, etc. on the earth or of the earth to cause what some believe was a 'chaos' or a judged earth resulting in its being formless and void (*tōhû wāḇōhû*).[4] There is so much read into these two verses by many commentators, it is not possible to deal with all of them. Verses from Job, Isaiah, Jeremiah, Ezekiel, Jude, II Peter, etc. as well as dinosaur space, many geological theories, various ages, man's sin and/or angelic sin, and much more are read back into Gen. 1:1-1:2 for a vast array of interpretations concerning creation. It is overwhelming how much data men read back into the creation account in Genesis. There is no need for this which just adds to the confusion resulting in a modern day chaos theory of Genesis 1:1-1:2. Why not just accept the simple rendering of His Word. He created the heavens and the earth ex-nihilo in 6 days and then rested on the 7th. "Thus the heavens and the earth were completed, and all their hosts. 2 And by the seventh day God completed His work which He had done; and He rested on the seventh day from all His work which He had done" (Gen. 2:1-2). He created and then rested on the 7th day from all His creation work. Of course one must believe this by faith.[5]

---

[4] As has been shown in Appendix A the expression (formless and void) has nothing to do with a judged earth or a judged anything in context.

[5] Hebrews 11:3 "**By faith** we understand that **the worlds** were prepared by the word of God, so that what is seen was not made out of things which are visible" Πίστει νοοῦμεν κατηρτίσθαι **τοὺς αἰῶνας** ῥήματι θεοῦ, εἰς τὸ μὴ ἐκ φαινομένων τὸ βλεπόμενον γεγονέναι. The ages include time, space, matter, living things, living creatures, and mankind. All this came into being

Scripture may be used to interpret Scripture not reinterpret the Scriptures. Everything in the Text supports a literal 6 days ex-nihilo creation, unless one reinterprets Gen. 1:1*ff*.

Isaiah 45:18

Isaiah 45:18 is used by many gap theorists to prove a gap theory i.e. some gap of time between Genesis 1:1 and 1:2 or a judgment prior to Genesis 1:1 known as 'the pre-creation chaos[6] theory.' What very few deal with in verse 45:18 is the actual construction of the verse from the Hebrew Text. The construction in this verse is so very important and significant.

The words created, formed, made, established, and more can all be used synonymously when dealing with the entire creation in Genesis 1:1 and following. Context is always going to be the key to determine primary meaning of any word (also see Appendix D).

> "For thus says the LORD, who **created** the heavens (He is the God who **formed** the earth and **made** it, He **established** it and did not **create it a waste place**,[7] *But* **formed** it to be inhabited), "I am the LORD, and there is none else" (Isaiah 45:18).

כִּי כֹה אָמַר־יְהוָה **בּוֹרֵא** הַשָּׁמַיִם
For thus says the LORD, who **created** the heavens
הוּא הָאֱלֹהִים **יֹצֵר** הָאָרֶץ **וְעֹשָׂהּ**
He is the God **who formed the earth and made it**,

---

from what had not yet appeared by the Son of God. And all was created by Him and for Him (Col. 1:16). He did not destroy His own creation and then recreate.

[6] It must be noted and kept in mind there are multiple creation theories, gap theories, and all kinds of speculation concerning creation.

[7] Isaiah 45:18 is critical as to the meaning of *tōhû* in context. As this was somewhat addressed in Appendix A, there is more which must be observed. In Genesis 1:1 it is very clear God created the heavens and the earth.

הוּא כוֹנְנָהּ
He established it
⁸לֹא־תֹהוּ בְרָאָהּ
not a waste place He **created** it
לָשֶׁבֶת יְצָרָהּ
to be inhabited He formed it
אֲנִי יְהוָה וְאֵין עוֹד׃
I am the LORD, and there is none else.

A crucial argument for most gap theories is the statement 'and He did not create it a waste place *tōhû* תֹהוּ.'⁹ This is read back into Gen. 1:1-2 which is used to prove the earth became a waste place or was a waste place and He recreated it. Does this really prove there was a gap between Gen. 1:1 and 1:2 (or before)?¹⁰

The Hebrew word for negation 'not' לֹא of 45:18, is used before the word *tōhû* לֹא־תֹהוּ 'not a waste place.' It is not before 'created it' בְרָאָהּ that is negating the verb. This is literally 'not formless He created it' לֹא־תֹהוּ בְרָאָהּ. The emphasis and negation is on the word תֹהוּ not the word created (it) בְרָאָהּ. The Text never said He created the earth to be formless or to remain formless.¹¹ Had this been the objective then the Text might have looked like this:

---

⁸ Note the negation לֹא here לֹא־תֹהוּ
⁹ Gap theorists argue that this proves He did not create a waste place but the earth or creation became a waste place or chaos. But are they reading Is. 45:18 correctly? So Moses and following generations would not know about this until Isaiah was written? Seems like quite a stretch.
¹⁰ Absolutely none of this proves any kind of a gap
¹¹ Literally this would be translated 'not formless(ness)' לֹא־תֹהוּ He created it (feminine singular) בְרָאָהּ (the earth).

תֹהוּ
בְּרֵאשִׁית בָּרָא אֱלֹהִים אֵת הָאָרֶץ.
In the beginning God created the earth a waste place or formless

But, this is not what the Text even hints at. The major emphasis is that the Creator has formed or made planet earth livable and productive for man.

לֹא־תֹהוּ בְרָאָהּ
not a **waste or formless** place He <u>**created**</u> it
לָשֶׁבֶת יְצָרָהּ
to be **inhabited** He <u>**formed**</u> it

not a **waste or formless** place He <u>**created**</u> it
to be **inhabited** He <u>**formed**</u> it

Make note of the construction in this verse. 'He created it' בְרָאָהּ is a qal perfect 3rd masculine singular with pronominal suffix. He created it not to be formless but to be inhabited. This is what the writer in Isaiah was emphasizing. This was not to be read back into Genesis 1:1*ff* as some commentary to reinterpret. There is enhancement to the creation account making it clear the earth was for habitation.[12]

God created man to rule over what He had created. This is easily supported and proves that this is the one and only creation God created, and never multiple creations or a recreation of anything. "Then God said, Let Us make man in Our image, according to Our likeness; and let them rule over the fish of the sea and over the birds of the sky and over the cattle and over all the earth, and over every creeping thing that creeps on the earth." (Gen 1:26). "When I consider Thy heavens, the work of Thy fingers, The moon and the stars, which Thou hast

---

[12] The act of creation was a total of 6 literal days, and the Text is very clear with this being documented by many other Texts.

ordained; ⁴ What is man, that Thou dost take thought of him? And the son of man, that Thou dost care for him? ⁵ Yet Thou hast made him a little lower than God, And dost crown him with glory and majesty! ⁶ Thou dost make him to rule over the works of Thy hands; Thou hast put all things under his feet, ⁷ All sheep and oxen, And also the beasts of the field, ⁸ The birds of the heavens, and the fish of the sea, Whatever passes through the paths of the seas. ⁹ O LORD, our Lord, How majestic is Thy name in all the earth!" (Ps. 8:3-9).

Everything was created ex-nihilo and flawless

Everything from Genesis 1:1 was created absolutely flawless. There were no errors and certainly no judgment/s; however the earth was not complete for human habitation. This will take a total of 6 literal 24 hour days. The earth needed to be fashioned and made livable for man so man could rule and reign with and under his Creator.

The Lord took 6 days to fashion His creation for man and then declared all which He created very good (Gen. 1:31).[13] He could not have said this had there been a previous destruction of His creation because of angels i.e. Satan and demons or another human race. How could He say all was very good when Satan and demons were/are still on the on the prowl ready to destroy (1 Pet. 5:8)[14], a coming flood in Genesis 6, and even the death of His Son, the Creator? All this to which God could say 'all was very good'? Everything was sinless and flawless in all God's creation when He said 'all was very good!' If Genesis 1*ff* is read as a complete unit without reinterpreting the Text with other Texts, science, archeology, geology, myths, men's theories, etc., then the Scripture easily teaches a literal ex-nihilo 6 day creation. And on the seventh

---

[13] "And God saw all that He had made, and behold, it was **very good**. And there was evening and there was morning, the sixth day" (Gen 1:31).
[14] "Be of sober *spirit*, be on the alert. Your adversary, the devil, prowls about like a roaring lion, seeking someone to devour" (1Pet. 5:8).

day, His creation was complete and *all* was very good.

Even a flawless diamond cannot be flawless unless found flawless from the start. Cutting a diamond may make it fit for some use, but it has to be 'formed or cut' yet it can only be flawless from the beginning. It cannot be made flawless by cutting or shaping it. What God did was flawless from the very beginning of creation. Everything He created from Gen. 1:1 until He rested was all done flawlessly with the creation account in Genesis with absolutely no catastrophes, judgments, or destructions. There is not one verse in all the Text to prove otherwise.

The fact God took 6 days to create, form, fashion, etc. is nothing for Him. He chose to make the planet less and less formless and more and more livable in those 6 days and then rested from His work of creation on the 7th day. And *all* was flawlessly good!

The Lord created one planet and the only one in His perfect creation with water[15] to sustain life. There may be others, but the Word records no other planet as such. He selected one planet out of all the billions of galaxies to form and fashion a program for man and to display His infinite glory, love, mercy, and grace which is ultimately displayed in His cross. All men are accountable for this biblical truth of the creation by the Creator. "For since the creation of the world His invisible attributes, His eternal power and divine nature, have been clearly seen, being understood through what has been made, so that they are without excuse" (Rom. 1:20).

Again, what is most significant is that all this can be easily shown or even proven by the construction of Isaiah 45:18.

לְשֶׁבֶת יְצָרָהּ   לֹא־תֹהוּ בְרָאָהּ

---

[15] As 'water' seems to be a problem with many commentators, it must be noted that the entire earth was covered with water. It is apparent there were no other planets covered with water as planet earth.

to be inhabited He formed **it** not formless He created **it**

Conclusion

There is absolutely no support for reading any other information back into Gen. 1:1*ff* to reinterpret these verses of His creation based on a supposed destruction of the planet using Isaiah 45:18 or any other verse or verses. Jesus never created a previous heaven, earth, ages and destroyed it and then recreated it. There is absolutely no proof for this in the Text. Jesus never created the heavens and earth to remain in a formless condition as the Text proves in context. *Not* a waste place or formless He created it *but* to be inhabited He formed it, "I am the LORD, and there is none else" (Is. 45:18). It must be continually kept in focus that the whole triune Godhead was involved in the creation yet 'all things were created by Him and for Him.'

The condition of the entire creation was flawless in Gen. 1:1 absolutely perfect! Sin had not yet entered His creation. Every planet might be called *tōhû wābōhû* but only earth was created to be inhabited and not formless or *tōhû*. The formlessness here or waste has only to do with the planet being unfit to inhabit by His creatures and specifically man. The earth was never created for angels in any sense let alone to inhabit. All Scriptures clearly teach a literal ex-nihilo 6 day creation from Genesis 1:1. On the 6th day He declared His creation and *all* that was in it to be very good (man and angels). Sin had not yet entered the creation in any sense up to 7th day.

Genesis 1:31 "And God saw all that He had made, and behold, it was **very good**. And there was evening and **there was morning, the sixth day**"

וַיַּרְא אֱלֹהִים אֶת־כָּל־אֲשֶׁר עָשָׂה וְהִנֵּה־טוֹב מְאֹד וַיְהִי־עֶרֶב וַיְהִי־בֹקֶר

יוֹם הַשִּׁשִּׁי:

Genesis 2:1 "Thus the heavens and the earth were **completed**, and all their hosts. ² And by **the seventh day** God completed His work which He had done; **and He rested on the seventh day from all His work which He had done**"

וַיְכֻלּוּ הַשָּׁמַיִם וְהָאָרֶץ וְכָל־צְבָאָם:

²וַיְכַל אֱלֹהִים בַּיּוֹם הַשְּׁבִיעִי מְלַאכְתּוֹ אֲשֶׁר עָשָׂה וַיִּשְׁבֹּת בַּיּוֹם הַשְּׁבִיעִי מִכָּל־מְלַאכְתּוֹ אֲשֶׁר עָשָׂה:

Appendix D

Create and made

Create בָּרָא and made עָשָׂה used synonymously

The verses which contain the words for create בָּרָא, and made עָשָׂה when referring to the Son's creation of the heavens and the earth may be used synonymously.[1] This is true when Genesis 1:1 is considered as an independent clause[2] denoting absolute ex nihilo creationism Genesis 1:1-2:3. The reason for this is that the Son of God created the one creation revealed in the Text. He never recreated any creation or previous creation as there is absolutely no biblical support for any of this.

There are those who hold various views of a recreation of a judged or destroyed creation either prior to Genesis 1:1 or just after. There is the gap theory and also the pre-creation chaos theory. And there are actually variations within these theories. Why not just believe that the Text is revealing one literal 6 day ex nihilo creation Genesis 1:1*ff*. Everything in the biblical Text accurately and invariably supports this view.

They make each word refer to completely separate events i.e. one for creation בָּרָא and the other for recreation עָשָׂה.[3] However to prove the various 'recreation' views, there is

---

[1] The verses which contain the words for create בָּרָא, made עָשָׂה when referring to the Son's creation of the heavens and the earth may be used synonymously. Other similar words may be included as formed יָצַר, fashioned, built, etc. The creation includes the heavens and the earth and all contained in them.

[2] A possible dependent clause would be 'when God created, when God began to create, when God began creation' or something similar, then the meaning of Genesis 1:1 would not be taken as an independent clause. Everything in the context proves this is nothing less than an independent clause.

[3] When Genesis 1:1 is understood as a dependent clause, then the meanings

usually a superficial distinction made between the words for 'create' בָּרָא and 'made' עָשָׂה.[4] Those who do not hold to the position that Genesis 1:1-2:3 is defining ex nihilo creationism typically make this total distinction between the meanings for create בָּרָא and made עָשָׂה actually ignoring basic lexical meanings, grammar, and context.

This appendix begins with a basic definition of these words and then their immediate or contextual use. The immediate context usage will always determine the precise meaning for these words and similar words referring to His creation. It is easy to prove biblically that the words for 'create' בָּרָא and 'made' עָשָׂה can be used synonymously for this present creation.

Basic lexical meanings for בָּרָא

BDB... בָּרָא ... shape, create ... Qal perfect Gn 1:1 ...imperfect יִבְרָא Gn 1:21, 27 Nu 16:30; ...*shape, fashion, create*, always of divine activity... object heaven and earth Gn 1:1; 2:3... Is 45:18, 18; mankind Gn 1:27...[5]

Gesenius... בָּרָא (1) TO CUT, TO CARVE OUT, TO FORM BY CUTTING ... (2) *to create, to produce*, ... Used of the creation of heaven and earth, Gen. 1:1; of men, Gen. 1:27; 5:1, 2; 6:7; specially Israel, Isa. 43:1, 15; Jer. 31:22, בָּרָא יְהוָה חֲדָשָׁה בָּאָרֶץ "the Lord has created a new thing in the earth, ... As to the passage, Gen. 2:3, בָּרָא לַעֲשׂוֹת should be explained "he produced by making," i.e. he made by producing something new.[6]

---

of these verbs cannot be used synonymously.
[4] Other similar words may also be included such as formed יָצַר, but the greatest artificial distinction which is basic to a creation then a recreation is between the words for **create** בָּרָא, and **made** עָשָׂה.
[5] Francis Brown, Samuel Rolles Driver, and Charles Augustus Briggs, *Enhanced Brown-Driver-Briggs Hebrew and English Lexicon* (Oxford: Clarendon Press, 1977), 135.
[6] Wilhelm Gesenius and Samuel Prideaux Tregelles, *Gesenius' Hebrew and*

Basic lexical meanings for עָשָׂה

BDB...עָשָׂה ... verb do, make... **b.** often of God's making (creating) Gn 3:1[7]

Gesenius...עָשָׂה ... TO LABOUR, TO WORK ABOUT ANYTHING...(2) *to make, to produce by labour* ...(*b*) used of God...*to produce, to create*, as heaven, earth, Gen. 1:7, 16; 2:2; 3:1; 5:1; 6:6; Ps. 96:5; 104:19. Hence עֹשֶׂה subst. *creator*, with suff. עֹשִׂי my creator, Job 35:10; עֹשֵׂהוּ his creator, Job 4:17; Isa. 17:7; 27:11; Hos. 8:14.[8]

The Scriptures begin with a simple independent clause stating fact.[9] The greatest issue is that one must take God's Word as inerrantly true.

Genesis 1:1 In the beginning God **created** the heavens and the earth.

בְּרֵאשִׁית **בָּרָא** אֱלֹהִים אֵת הַשָּׁמַיִם וְאֵת הָאָרֶץ׃

There are many verses revealing God **made** the heavens, the earth, the seas, man, the angelic realm, etc: Gen. 2:4; Ex. 20:11; 31:17; 2 Kings 19:15; 2 Chr. 2:12; Neh. 9:6; Ps. 121:2; 124:8; 134:3; 146:6; Isa. 37:16; Acts 14:15; 17:24; Rev. 14:7.

Chaldee Lexicon to the Old Testament Scriptures (Bellingham, WA: Logos Bible Software, 2003), 138–139.

[7] Francis Brown, Samuel Rolles Driver, and Charles Augustus Briggs, *Enhanced Brown-Driver-Briggs Hebrew and English Lexicon* (Oxford: Clarendon Press, 1977), 793–795.

[8] Wilhelm Gesenius and Samuel Prideaux Tregelles, *Gesenius' Hebrew and Chaldee Lexicon to the Old Testament Scriptures* (Bellingham, WA: Logos Bible Software, 2003), 657–658.

[9] It must be continually noted that when Genesis 1:1 is understood as a dependent clause, then the meanings of these verbs cannot be used synonymously.

Several verses are presented here not only showing the making of the heavens and the earth but *all* they contain:

1. He made '*the sea and all that is in them*' (Ex. 20:11; Neh. 9:6; Ps. 146:6)
2. He made the angelic realm '*the heaven of heavens with all their host*' (Neh. 9:6)

Psalm 146:6 Who <u>**made**</u> heaven and earth, The sea and all that is in them; Who keeps faith forever.

עֹשֶׂה׀ שָׁמַיִם וָאָרֶץ אֶת־הַיָּם וְאֶת־כָּל־אֲשֶׁר־בָּם הַשֹּׁמֵר אֱמֶת לְעוֹלָם׃

Exodus 20:11 For in six days the LORD <u>**made**</u> the heavens and the earth, the <u>sea and all that is in them</u>, and rested on the seventh day; therefore the LORD blessed the sabbath day and made it holy.

כִּי שֵׁשֶׁת־יָמִים עָשָׂה יְהוָה אֶת־הַשָּׁמַיִם וְאֶת־הָאָרֶץ אֶת־הַיָּם וְאֶת־כָּל־אֲשֶׁר־בָּם וַיָּנַח בַּיּוֹם הַשְּׁבִיעִי עַל־כֵּן בֵּרַךְ יְהוָה אֶת־יוֹם הַשַּׁבָּת וַיְקַדְּשֵׁהוּ׃ ס

From Genesis 1:1 to Revelation there is not a hint in all the Word that the Son of God created the heavens, earth, seas, all living things and creatures , eons[10], etc, and then recreated anything or everything. This would mean He also recreated the angelic realm in which sin originated? If sin had already occurred in the angelic realm, it is hard to believe God could say all was 'very good' in Gen. 1:31. This would be especially true where the true battle of sin will be for the seed of the woman to conquer or crush the serpent's head (Gen. 3:15).

No recreation theory can be supported biblically. Most of this confusion stems from the belief that the words for

---

[10]This is the ages or eons referred to in Heb. 1:2 and 11:3; "In these last days has spoken to us in *His* Son, whom He appointed heir of all things, through whom also He made the world." (Heb 1:2). The Son created the ages and all they contain.

create בָּרָא is one event and the word for made עָשָׂה is another event.

<u>words create</u> בָּרָא =
creation
<u>and made</u> עָשָׂה =
recreation

The words created and made in the same verse

Note that in Gen. 2:3 and 2:4 'created בָּרָא and made עָשָׂה' are both used in the same verses. This is very significant for those who want to stress an absolute distinction between these two words.

Genesis 2:3 Then God blessed the seventh day and sanctified it, because in it He rested from all His work which God had **created and made**.

וַיְבָרֶךְ אֱלֹהִים אֶת־יוֹם הַשְּׁבִיעִי וַיְקַדֵּשׁ אֹתוֹ כִּי בוֹ שָׁבַת מִכָּל־מְלַאכְתּוֹ אֲשֶׁר־**בָּרָא** אֱלֹהִים **לַעֲשׂוֹת**:

Genesis 2:4 This is the account of the heavens and the earth when they were **created**, in the day that the LORD God **made** earth and heaven.

אֵלֶּה תוֹלְדוֹת הַשָּׁמַיִם וְהָאָרֶץ **בְּהִבָּרְאָם** בְּיוֹם **עֲשׂוֹת** יְהוָה אֱלֹהִים אֶרֶץ וְשָׁמָיִם:

Gesenius made this comment on Genesis 2:3. "As to the passage, Gen. 2:3, בָּרָא לַעֲשׂוֹת should be explained "he produced by making," i.e. he made by producing something new."[11] The comment is very sobering as God created by

---

[11] Wilhelm Gesenius and Samuel Prideaux Tregelles, <u>Gesenius' Hebrew and Chaldee Lexicon to the Old Testament Scriptures</u> (Bellingham, WA: Logos Bible Software, 2003), 138–139.

making something i.e. created that which was made. The two words are thusly joined as the Text proves. So the result of the creation is that which was made, precisely all which the Son of God made. There is absolutely no possibility of making the creation as the work of God totally distinct from that which He made. To make this unnatural distinction is to disregard basic lexical meanings and ignore fundamental exegetical methodology simply to prove some theory.

Paul makes a very cogent point about His creation which He made. "For since the **creation** of the world His invisible attributes, His eternal power and divine nature, have been clearly seen, being understood through what has been **made**, so that they are without excuse" τὰ γὰρ ἀόρατα αὐτοῦ ἀπὸ **κτίσεως** κόσμου τοῖς **ποιήμασιν** νοούμενα καθορᾶται, ἥ τε ἀΐδιος αὐτοῦ δύναμις καὶ θειότης, εἰς τὸ εἶναι αὐτοὺς ἀναπολογήτους (Rom. 1:20).

There are other verses which have both create and made used synonymously within the same verse and other words also used synonymously.

Genesis 6:7 And the LORD said, "I will blot out man whom I have **created** from the face of the land, from man to animals to creeping things and to birds of the sky; for I am sorry that I have **made** them."

וַיֹּאמֶר יְהוָה אֶמְחֶה אֶת־הָאָדָם **אֲשֶׁר־בָּרָאתִי** מֵעַל פְּנֵי הָאֲדָמָה מֵאָדָם עַד־בְּהֵמָה עַד־רֶמֶשׂ וְעַד־עוֹף הַשָּׁמָיִם כִּי נִחַמְתִּי כִּי **עֲשִׂיתִם**׃

Isaiah 43:7 Everyone who is called by My name, And whom I have **created** for My glory, Whom I have **formed**, even whom I have **made**.

כֹּל הַנִּקְרָא בִשְׁמִי וְלִכְבוֹדִי **בְּרָאתִיו** יְצַרְתִּיו אַף־**עֲשִׂיתִיו**׃

Isaiah 45:12 It is I who **made** the earth, and **created** man upon it. I **stretched** out the heavens with My hands, And I **ordained** all their host.

אָנֹכִי **עָשִׂיתִי** אֶרֶץ וְאָדָם עָלֶיהָ **בָרָאתִי** אֲנִי יָדַי **נָטוּ** שָׁמַיִם וְכָל־צְבָאָם **צִוֵּיתִי**׃

Isaiah 45:18 For thus says the LORD, who **created** the heavens (He is the God who **formed** the earth and **made** it, He **established** it and did not **create** it a waste place, *But* **formed** it to be inhabited), "I am the LORD, and there is none else.

כִּי כֹה אָמַר־יְהוָה **בּוֹרֵא** הַשָּׁמַיִם הוּא הָאֱלֹהִים **יֹצֵר** הָאָרֶץ **וְעֹשָׂהּ** הוּא כוֹנְנָהּ לֹא־תֹהוּ **בְרָאָהּ** לָשֶׁבֶת יְצָרָהּ אֲנִי יְהוָה וְאֵין עוֹד:

There are many verses which prove that the words 'create and made' are used synonymously and should not be understood as separate acts of God. No matter what, context is always going to be the key for meaning and interpretation. What lengths many will go to prove something which is nothing more than reducing the Text to very strange doctrines that merely create speculation.

God's creative work made the 7 day week

God's creative work ceased on the 6th day and He rested on the 7th day. This originated man's complete time system (God's created time which He made) based on the entire creation being made and completed on the 6th day. This was not a recreation nor was it recreated according to the Text. There is nothing to prove anything else but one literal 6 day creation making a literal 7 day week.[12] Man's time system i.e. literal time as man knows it (day and night, a 24 hour day, 7 day week, sun and planets all created and associated with this same created time) is totally based on a literal 6 day creation. Again, time was created by what He had made.

Genesis 2:2 And by the seventh day God completed His work which He had **done**; and He rested on the seventh day from all

---

[12] No one can prove any literal time system in a previous creation. If He recreated a 7 day universal time system, there is absolutely no biblical proof for any of this.

His work which He **had done**.

וַיְכַל אֱלֹהִים בַּיּוֹם הַשְּׁבִיעִי מְלַאכְתּוֹ אֲשֶׁר **עָשָׂה** וַיִּשְׁבֹּת בַּיּוֹם הַשְּׁבִיעִי מִכָּל־מְלַאכְתּוֹ אֲשֶׁר **עָשָׂה**׃

Exodus 20:11 For in six days the LORD **made** the heavens and the earth, the sea and all that is in them, and rested on the seventh day; therefore the LORD blessed the sabbath day and made it holy.

כִּי שֵׁשֶׁת־יָמִים **עָשָׂה** יְהוָה אֶת־הַשָּׁמַיִם וְאֶת־הָאָרֶץ אֶת־הַיָּם וְאֶת־כָּל־אֲשֶׁר־בָּם וַיָּנַח בַּיּוֹם הַשְּׁבִיעִי עַל־כֵּן בֵּרַךְ יְהוָה אֶת־יוֹם הַשַּׁבָּת וַיְקַדְּשֵׁהוּ׃

Exodus 31:17 It is a sign between Me and the sons of Israel forever; for in six days the LORD **made** heaven and earth, but on the seventh day He ceased *from labor*, and was refreshed."

בֵּינִי וּבֵין בְּנֵי יִשְׂרָאֵל אוֹת הִוא לְעֹלָם כִּי־שֵׁשֶׁת יָמִים **עָשָׂה** יְהוָה אֶת־הַשָּׁמַיִם וְאֶת־הָאָרֶץ וּבַיּוֹם הַשְּׁבִיעִי שָׁבַת וַיִּנָּפַשׁ׃

The creation of *man* using the words create, made, and formed synonymously

Genesis 1:27 And God **created** man in His own image, in the image of God He **created** him; male and female He **created** them.

וַיִּבְרָא אֱלֹהִים ׀ אֶת־הָאָדָם בְּצַלְמוֹ בְּצֶלֶם אֱלֹהִים **בָּרָא** אֹתוֹ זָכָר וּנְקֵבָה **בָּרָא** אֹתָם׃

Genesis 2:7 Then the LORD God **formed** man of dust from the ground, and breathed into his nostrils the breath of life; and man became a living being.

וַיִּיצֶר יְהוָה אֱלֹהִים אֶת־הָאָדָם עָפָר מִן־הָאֲדָמָה וַיִּפַּח בְּאַפָּיו נִשְׁמַת חַיִּים וַיְהִי הָאָדָם לְנֶפֶשׁ חַיָּה׃

Genesis 2:8 And the LORD God planted a garden toward the east, in Eden; and there He placed the man whom He had **formed**.

וַיִּטַּע יְהוָה אֱלֹהִים גַּן־בְּעֵדֶן מִקֶּדֶם וַיָּשֶׂם שָׁם אֶת־הָאָדָם אֲשֶׁר **יָצָר**׃

Genesis 5:1 This is the book of the generations of Adam. In the day when God **created** man, He **made** him in the likeness of God.

זֶה סֵפֶר תּוֹלְדֹת אָדָם בְּיוֹם **בְּרֹא** אֱלֹהִים אָדָם בִּדְמוּת אֱלֹהִים **עָשָׂה** אֹתוֹ׃

Genesis 5:2 He **created** them male and female, and He blessed them and named them Man in the day when they were **created**.

זָכָר וּנְקֵבָה **בְּרָאָם** וַיְבָרֶךְ אֹתָם וַיִּקְרָא אֶת־שְׁמָם אָדָם בְּיוֹם **הִבָּרְאָם**׃

Genesis 6:7 And the LORD said, "I will blot out man whom I have **created** from the face of the land, from man to animals to creeping things and to birds of the sky; for I am sorry that I have **made** them."

וַיֹּאמֶר יְהוָה אֶמְחֶה אֶת־הָאָדָם אֲשֶׁר־**בָּרָאתִי** מֵעַל פְּנֵי הָאֲדָמָה מֵאָדָם עַד־בְּהֵמָה עַד־רֶמֶשׂ וְעַד־עוֹף הַשָּׁמָיִם כִּי נִחַמְתִּי כִּי **עֲשִׂיתִם**׃

Isaiah 43:7 Everyone who is called by My name, And whom I have **created** for My glory, Whom I have **formed**, even whom I have **made**."

כֹּל הַנִּקְרָא בִשְׁמִי וְלִכְבוֹדִי **בְּרָאתִיו יְצַרְתִּיו אַף־עֲשִׂיתִיו**׃

Isaiah 45:12 "It is I who **made** the earth, and **created** man upon it. I stretched out the heavens with My hands, And I ordained all their host.

אָנֹכִי **עָשִׂיתִי** אֶרֶץ וְאָדָם עָלֶיהָ **בָרָאתִי** אֲנִי יָדַי נָטוּ שָׁמַיִם וְכָל־צְבָאָם צִוֵּיתִי׃

Psalm 89:47 Remember what my span of life is; For what vanity Thou hast **created** all the sons of men!

זְכָר־אֲנִי מֶה־חָלֶד עַל־מַה־שָּׁוְא **בָּרָאתָ** כָל־בְּנֵי־אָדָם׃

Matthew 19:4 And He answered and said, "Have you not read, that He who **created** them from the beginning **made** them male and female ὁ δὲ ἀποκριθεὶς εἶπεν· οὐκ ἀνέγνωτε ὅτι ὁ **κτίσας** ἀπ' ἀρχῆς ἄρσεν καὶ θῆλυ **ἐποίησεν** αὐτούς;

Mark 10:6 But from the **beginning of creation**, God **made** them male and female. ἀπὸ δὲ **ἀρχῆς κτίσεως** ἄρσεν καὶ θῆλυ **ἐποίησεν** αὐτούς·

The creation of the animal world using the words create, made, and formed synonymously

Genesis 1:21 And God **created** the great sea monsters, and every living creature that moves, with which the waters swarmed after their kind, and every winged bird after its kind; and God saw that it was good.

וַיִּבְרָ֣א אֱלֹהִ֔ים אֶת־הַתַּנִּינִ֖ם הַגְּדֹלִ֑ים וְאֵ֣ת כָּל־נֶ֣פֶשׁ הַֽחַיָּ֣ה׀ הָֽרֹמֶ֡שֶׂת אֲשֶׁר֩ שָׁרְצ֨וּ הַמַּ֜יִם לְמִֽינֵהֶ֗ם וְאֵ֨ת כָּל־ע֤וֹף כָּנָף֙ לְמִינֵ֔הוּ וַיַּ֥רְא אֱלֹהִ֖ים כִּי־טֽוֹב׃

Genesis 1:25 And God **made** the beasts of the earth after their kind, and the cattle after their kind, and everything that creeps on the ground after its kind; and God saw that it was good.

וַיַּ֣עַשׂ אֱלֹהִים֩ אֶת־חַיַּ֨ת הָאָ֜רֶץ לְמִינָ֗הּ וְאֶת־הַבְּהֵמָה֙ לְמִינָ֔הּ וְאֵ֛ת כָּל־רֶ֥מֶשׂ הָֽאֲדָמָ֖ה לְמִינֵ֑הוּ וַיַּ֥רְא אֱלֹהִ֖ים כִּי־טֽוֹב׃

Genesis 2:19 And out of the ground the LORD God **formed** every beast of the field and every bird of the sky, and brought *them* to the man to see what he would call them; and whatever the man called a living creature, that was its name.

וַיִּצֶר֩ יְהוָ֨ה אֱלֹהִ֜ים מִן־הָֽאֲדָמָ֗ה כָּל־חַיַּ֤ת הַשָּׂדֶה֙ וְאֵת֙ כָּל־ע֣וֹף הַשָּׁמַ֔יִם וַיָּבֵא֙ אֶל־הָ֣אָדָ֔ם לִרְא֖וֹת מַה־יִּקְרָא־ל֑וֹ וְכֹל֩ אֲשֶׁ֨ר יִקְרָא־ל֧וֹ הָֽאָדָ֛ם נֶ֥פֶשׁ חַיָּ֖ה ה֥וּא שְׁמֽוֹ׃

Genesis 3:1 Now the serpent was more crafty than any beast of the field which the LORD God had **made**. And he said to the woman, "Indeed, has God said, 'You shall not eat from any tree of the garden '?"

וְהַנָּחָשׁ֙ הָיָ֣ה עָר֔וּם מִכֹּל֙ חַיַּ֣ת הַשָּׂדֶ֔ה אֲשֶׁ֥ר **עָשָׂ֖ה** יְהוָ֣ה אֱלֹהִ֑ים וַיֹּ֙אמֶר֙ אֶל־הָ֣אִשָּׁ֔ה אַ֚ף כִּֽי־אָמַ֣ר אֱלֹהִ֔ים לֹ֣א תֹֽאכְל֔וּ מִכֹּ֖ל עֵ֥ץ הַגָּֽן׃

Genesis 6:7 And the LORD said, "I will blot out man whom I have **created** from the face of the land, from **man to animals to creeping things and to birds of the sky**; for I am sorry that I have **made** them."

וַיֹּ֣אמֶר יְהוָ֗ה אֶמְחֶ֨ה אֶת־הָאָדָ֤ם אֲשֶׁר־**בָּרָ֙אתִי֙** מֵעַל֙ פְּנֵ֣י הָֽאֲדָמָ֔ה מֵֽאָדָם֙ עַד־בְּהֵמָ֔ה עַד־רֶ֖מֶשׂ וְעַד־ע֣וֹף הַשָּׁמָ֑יִם כִּ֥י נִחַ֖מְתִּי כִּ֥י **עֲשִׂיתִֽם**׃

Psalm 146:6 Who **made heaven** and **earth**, The **sea** and **all that is in them**; Who keeps faith forever;

עֹשֶׂ֤ה׀ שָׁמַ֣יִם וָ֭אָרֶץ אֶת־הַיָּ֥ם וְאֶת־כָּל־אֲשֶׁר־בָּ֑ם הַשֹּׁמֵ֖ר אֱמֶ֣ת לְעוֹלָֽם׃

<u>Note also that the words for Maker[13] and Creator[14] may also be used synonymously</u>

Isaiah 40:28 Do you not know? Have you not heard? The Everlasting God, the LORD, the **Creator** of the ends of the earth does not become weary or tired. His understanding is inscrutable.

הֲל֨וֹא יָדַ֜עְתָּ אִם־לֹ֣א שָׁמַ֗עְתָּ אֱלֹהֵ֨י עוֹלָ֤ם׀ יְהוָה֙ **בּוֹרֵא֙** קְצ֣וֹת הָאָ֔רֶץ לֹ֥א יִיעַ֖ף וְלֹ֣א יִיגָ֑ע אֵ֥ין חֵ֖קֶר לִתְבוּנָתֽוֹ׃

Psalm 115:15 May you be blessed of the LORD, **Maker** of heaven and earth.

---

[13] Ps. 95:6, 115:15, 149:2; Prov. 14:31, 17:5; Isa. 17:7, 27:11, 44:24, 45:9, 11, 51:13, 54:5; Jer. 10:16, 51:19, 8:14.
[14] Eccl. 12:1; Isa. 27:11; Isa. 40:28; Isa. 43:1, 15; Rom. 1:25; 1 Pet. 4:19.

בְּרוּכִים אַתֶּם לַיהוָה **עֹשֵׂה** שָׁמַיִם וָאָרֶץ:

The word for made עָשָׂה does not have the meaning that the creation was recreated. There will be a new creation, a regeneration[15] not a recreation.

The creation of the heavens and their host (the angelic realm) using the words create and made synonymously

Nehemiah 9:6 Thou alone art the LORD. Thou hast **made** the heavens, the heaven of heavens **with all their host**, The earth and all that is on it, The seas and all that is in them. Thou dost give life to all of them and **the heavenly host bows down before Thee**.

אַתָּה־הוּא יְהוָה לְבַדֶּךָ (אַתְּ) [אַתָּה] **עָשִׂיתָ** אֶת־הַשָּׁמַיִם שְׁמֵי הַשָּׁמַיִם וְכָל־צְבָאָם הָאָרֶץ וְכָל־אֲשֶׁר עָלֶיהָ הַיַּמִּים וְכָל־אֲשֶׁר בָּהֶם וְאַתָּה מְחַיֶּה אֶת־כֻּלָּם וּצְבָא הַשָּׁמַיִם לְךָ מִשְׁתַּחֲוִים:

Psalm 33:6 By the word of the LORD the heavens were **made**, And by the breath of His mouth **all their host**.

בִּדְבַר יְהוָה שָׁמַיִם **נַעֲשׂוּ** וּבְרוּחַ פִּיו כָּל־צְבָאָם:

Psalm 148:1 Praise the LORD! Praise the LORD from the heavens; Praise Him in the heights! [2] Praise Him, **all His angels**; Praise Him, **all His hosts**! [3] Praise Him, sun and moon; Praise Him, all stars of light! [4] Praise Him, highest heavens, and the waters that are above the heavens! [5] Let them praise the name of the LORD, For He commanded and **they were created**.

---

[15] "And Jesus said to them, Truly I say to you, that you who have followed Me, **in the regeneration** when the Son of Man will sit on His glorious throne, you also shall sit upon twelve thrones, judging the twelve tribes of Israel" (Mat. 19:28).

הַלְלוּ יָהּ הַלְלוּ אֶת־יְהוָה מִן־הַשָּׁמַיִם הַלְלוּהוּ בַּמְּרוֹמִים: ² הַלְלוּהוּ כָל־מַלְאָכָיו הַלְלוּהוּ כָּל־(צְבָאוֹ) [צְבָאָיו]: ³ הַלְלוּהוּ שֶׁמֶשׁ וְיָרֵחַ הַלְלוּהוּ כָּל־כּוֹכְבֵי אוֹר: ⁴ הַלְלוּהוּ שְׁמֵי הַשָּׁמָיִם וְהַמַּיִם אֲשֶׁר ׀ מֵעַל הַשָּׁמָיִם: ⁵ יְהַלְלוּ אֶת־שֵׁם יְהוָה כִּי הוּא צִוָּה וְנִבְרָאוּ:

The Psalmist is calling for the entire heavenly host, the angels, and all creation to praise the name of the Lord. These verses reveal the earth and the heavens with all their hosts were created i.e. made (both words being used interchangeably). There was no possibility of a recreation especially of the angelic realm.

This is the same creation as we know it, never recreated.

Revelation 5:13 And every **created thing** which is in heaven **and on the earth and under the earth and on the sea, and all things in them**, I heard saying, "To Him who sits on the throne, and to the Lamb, *be* blessing and honor and glory and dominion forever and ever. καὶ **πᾶν κτίσμα** ὃ ἐν τῷ οὐρανῷ καὶ ἐπὶ τῆς γῆς καὶ ὑποκάτω τῆς γῆς καὶ ἐπὶ τῆς θαλάσσης καὶ τὰ ἐν αὐτοῖς πάντα ἤκουσα λέγοντας· τῷ καθημένῳ ἐπὶ τῷ θρόνῳ καὶ τῷ ἀρνίῳ ἡ εὐλογία καὶ ἡ τιμὴ καὶ ἡ δόξα καὶ τὸ κράτος εἰς τοὺς αἰῶνας τῶν αἰώνων.

Revelation 10:6 and swore by Him who lives forever and ever, who **created heaven and the things in it, and the earth and the things in it, and the sea and the things in it**, that there shall be delay no longer καὶ ὤμοσεν ἐν τῷ ζῶντι εἰς τοὺς αἰῶνας τῶν αἰώνων, ὃς **ἔκτισεν τὸν οὐρανὸν καὶ τὰ ἐν αὐτῷ καὶ τὴν γῆν καὶ τὰ ἐν αὐτῇ καὶ τὴν θάλασσαν καὶ τὰ ἐν αὐτῇ**, ὅτι χρόνος οὐκέτι ἔσται,

Conclusion

The words for create בָּרָא and made עָשָׂה can be used synonymously throughout the entire Text. The words are used synonymously for creation even in the same verses. They also can be used synonymously for time as a 7 day week, used synonymously for the creation of man and animals, and used synonymously in both the Hebrew and Greek Texts.

It must be constantly reminded that all things were created by Him, the Son of God and for Him. There is nothing in the Text that anything was recreated by Him and for Him (Col. 1:16). The believer's help comes from his Creator Who made the heaven and the earth.

Psalm 121:2 My help *comes* from the LORD, Who **made heaven** and **earth**.

עֶזְרִי מֵעִם יְהוָה **עֹשֵׂה** שָׁמַיִם וָאָרֶץ׃

Genesis 1:1 In the beginning God **created** the heavens and the earth.

בְּרֵאשִׁית **בָּרָא** אֱלֹהִים אֵת הַשָּׁמַיִם וְאֵת הָאָרֶץ׃

True faith rests upon the inerrant Word of God. It is all by faith we believe God and take Him at His Word.

> "In the beginning God created the heavens and the earth" (Gen 1:1). "In these last days has spoken to us in *His* Son, whom He appointed heir of all things, through whom also He made the world" (Heb 1:2). "**By faith** we understand that the worlds were prepared by the word of God, so that what is seen was not made out of things which are visible" (Heb. 11:3).

Again, the words for create בָּרָא and made עָשָׂה referring in context to the Son's creation are used synonymously.

Appendix E

Hebrews 1:2 and 11:3

Hebrews 1:2 and Hebrews 11:3 truly prove the Son of God is not only the Creator, but He spoke the entire creation into existence by His word. All this proves His ex nihilo creation. This appendix will consider Hebrews 1:2 and 11:3 by observing basic lexical meanings and their usage in context.

Hebrews 1:2

Hebrews 1:2 in these last days has spoken to us in *His* Son, whom He appointed heir of all things, through whom also He **made** the **world**. ἐπ' ἐσχάτου τῶν ἡμερῶν τούτων ἐλάλησεν ἡμῖν ἐν υἱῷ, ὃν ἔθηκεν κληρονόμον πάντων, δι' οὗ καὶ **ἐποίησεν** τοὺς **αἰῶνας**·

Lexical meanings

αἰών, ῶνος, ὁ ... **a long period of time, without reference to beginning or end**... of time to come which, if it has no end, is also known as *eternity* ... **the world as a spatial concept,** *the world* ...Created by God through the Son **Hb 1:2**; through God's word **11:3**. Hence God is βασιλεὺς τῶν αἰ. **1 Ti 1:17; Rv 15:3;**[1]

ποιέω ...I. active—1. *do, make*—a. of external things *make, manufacture, produce* ...β. of God's creative activity *create* ... In LXX often for בָּרָא [2]

---

[1] William Arndt, Frederick W. Danker, and Walter Bauer, *A Greek-English Lexicon of the New Testament and Other Early Christian Literature* (Chicago: University of Chicago Press, 2000), 32–33.
[2] William Arndt, F. Wilbur Gingrich, Frederick W. Danker, et al., *A Greek-English Lexicon of the New Testament and Other Early Christian Literature : A Translation and Adaption of the Fourth Revised and Augmented Edition of Walter Bauer's Griechisch-Deutsches Worterbuch Zu Den Schrift En Des*

Note that ποιέω 'do or make' can easily be used of God's activities in His creation through the Son. Examples of the definition and use of ποιέω are following (including the LXX, in the LXX ποιέω is often used for בָּרָא):

Genesis 1:1 In the beginning God <u>**created**</u> the heavens and the earth. (LXX) ἐν ἀρχῇ <u>**ἐποίησεν**</u> ὁ θεὸς τὸν οὐρανὸν καὶ τὴν γῆν
בְּרֵאשִׁית **בָּרָא** אֱלֹהִים אֵת הַשָּׁמַיִם וְאֵת הָאָרֶץ׃

Genesis 1:27 And God <u>**created**</u> man in His own image, in the image of God He created him; male and female He <u>**created**</u> them. (LXX) καὶ <u>**ἐποίησεν**</u> ὁ θεὸς τὸν ἄνθρωπον κατ᾽ εἰκόνα θεοῦ <u>**ἐποίησεν**</u> αὐτόν ἄρσεν καὶ θῆλυ <u>**ἐποίησεν**</u> αὐτούς
וַיִּבְרָא אֱלֹהִים ׀ אֶת־הָאָדָם בְּצַלְמוֹ בְּצֶלֶם אֱלֹהִים **בָּרָא** אֹתוֹ זָכָר וּנְקֵבָה **בָּרָא** אֹתָם׃

Genesis 5:1 This is the book of the generations of Adam. In the day when God <u>**created**</u> man, He <u>**made**</u> him in the likeness of God. (LXX) αὕτη ἡ βίβλος γενέσεως ἀνθρώπων ᾗ ἡμέρᾳ <u>**ἐποίησεν**</u> ὁ θεὸς τὸν Αδαμ κατ᾽ εἰκόνα θεοῦ <u>**ἐποίησεν**</u> αὐτόν
זֶה סֵפֶר תּוֹלְדֹת אָדָם בְּיוֹם **בְּרֹא** אֱלֹהִים אָדָם בִּדְמוּת אֱלֹהִים **עָשָׂה** אֹתוֹ׃

The Scriptures and especially Hebrews are exceptionally clear that the Son is the Heir of all things as well as the Creator of all things. This heirship almost takes precedent over the act of His creation i.e. creating everything i.e. the world, the ages, time, space, matter, angels, and more, literally everything. He is presented here as the Heir first and then the Creator. As the Creator, this will be discussed more in Hebrews 11:3.

Neuen Testaments Und Der Ubrigen Urchristlichen Literatur (Chicago: University of Chicago Press, 1979), 680–682.

He is the Heir of all created things which He Himself created. 'Made the world or ages' is actually more than just the created elements of time, space, matter, and life which He created. "To begin with (v. 2b), the Son is the designated **Heir of all things**. This is obviously as it should be since He is also their Maker—the One **through whom He made the universe** (*tous aiōnas*, lit., "the ages," also rendered "the universe" in 11:3). The reference to the Son's heirship anticipates the thought of His future reign, of which the writer will say much. But the One who is both Creator and Heir is also a perfect reflection of the God who has spoken in Him. Moreover **His Word** is so **powerful** that all He has made is sustained by that Word. And it is this Person who has **provided purification for sins** and taken His seat **at the right hand of the Majesty in heaven** (cf. 8:1; 10:12; 12:2). In doing so it is obvious He has attained an eminence far beyond anything **the angels** can claim."[3]

The Son literally created the ages which include all the elements and living things of creation and much more. The ages are the eons of creation which some designate as the world/s or universe. "Thus already at the beginning God made the eons 'through Him' namely with a view to the Son's being the heir in the fullness of time to have the vast inheritance as a man. Ποιεῖν is the same as *barah* (Gen. 1:1), to bring into being. 'All things διὰ αὐτοῦ (the same phrase) ἐγένετο, through him came into existence; and without him there came into existence not a single thing that has come into existence (and thus exists), John 1:3."[4] Absolutely nothing has existed prior to the creation by the Son of God. He is the Agent of all creation and Hebrews 1:2 makes this very clear. And the writer of Hebrews emphasizes this even more in Hebrews 11:3.

---

[3] Zane C. Hodges, "Hebrews," in *The Bible Knowledge Commentary: An Exposition of the Scriptures*, ed. J. F. Walvoord and R. B. Zuck, vol. 2 (Wheaton, IL: Victor Books, 1985), 780–781.
[4] R. C. H. Lenski, '*The Interpretation of the Epistle to the Hebrews and the Epistle of James*' (Minneapolis, Minnesota: Augsburg Publishing House, 1066), p. 35.

Hebrews 11:3

Hebrews 11:3 By faith we understand that the **worlds** were **prepared** by the word of God, so that what is seen was not made out of things which are visible. Πίστει νοοῦμεν **κατηρτίσθαι** τοὺς **αἰῶνας** ῥήματι θεοῦ, εἰς τὸ μὴ ἐκ φαινομένων τὸ βλεπόμενον γεγονέναι.

Lexical meanings

καταρτίζω …to cause to be in a condition to function well, *put in order, restore*… to prepare for a purpose, *prepare, make, create, outfit*… active and passive of God (w. ποιεῖν) …ῥήματι θεοῦ **Hb 11:3**. κατηρτισμένος εἴς τι *made, created for something* [5]

    Jesus, as the Son of God did more than restore things, and there is no record of any of this 'being recreated' in the Word. What is made very clear is that all that was created i.e. the ages and all they contain was created through the Son (Heb. 1:2). He did this by His word when He spoke all creation into existence, and all this out of nothing that preexisted. This not only proves creation by Him 'ex nihilo,' but all the ages and all contained in those ages of creation has purpose. The basic meaning of καταρτίζω here is not only to prepare for a purpose, but was created for divine purpose/s. Everything in creation that He created by His word has rationale and function.

    But, what is literally seen by man is the result of what has come out or been spoken out of nothing by the eternal Son. All creation and the ages proceeded from nothing that preexisted. "The result of this creation by an unseen force, the

---

[5] William Arndt, Frederick W. Danker, and Walter Bauer, *A Greek-English Lexicon of the New Testament and Other Early Christian Literature* (Chicago: University of Chicago Press, 2000), 526.

word of God, is that what is seen has not come into being out of things which appear.. εἰς τὸ …γεγονέναι… εἰς τὸ with infinitive, commonly used to express purpose, is sometimes as here used to express result, and we may legitimately translate 'so that was is seen, etc'[6]… Had the visible world been formed out of materials which were subject to human observation, there would have been no need for faith. Science could have traced it to its origin. Evolution only pushes the statement a stage back.'[7] What is seen or observed in this creation did not come about from anything that preexisted or had appeared. The result of His speaking was this creation spoken into existence in 6 literal days (Genesis 1:1-2:3; Hebrews 1:2 and 11:3).

Conclusion

The Son spoke the entire creation into existence. Hebrew 1:2 and 11:3 prove the Son of God is not only the Heir of all creation, but He spoke the entire creation and all it contains into existence by His word.[8] He spoke and the result was the entire creation in six days. The Scriptures are very clear on literal, ex nihilo creationism from Genesis 1:1*ff*, Hebrews 1:2 and 11:3.

---

[6] The writer is confirming the validity of the translation i.e. 'so that what is seen' verifying result. "By faith we understand that the worlds were prepared by the word of God, **so that what is seen** was not made out of things which are visible" (Heb. 11:3). Πίστει νοοῦμεν κατηρτίσθαι τοὺς αἰῶνας ῥήματι θεοῦ, **εἰς τὸ** μὴ ἐκ φαινομένων τὸ βλεπόμενον **γεγονέναι**. The writer is validating that what is seen in creation did not come from anything previously manifested or visible. It was all spoken into existence by Him, and this is made very clear in the Text.

[7] W. Robertson Nicoll, *The Expositors Greek Testament*, Volume IV (Grand Rapids: WM. B. Eerdmans Publishing Company, 1967), p. 353.

[8] Jesus as the Son of God spoke the entire creation into existence from nothing. The Text is perfectly clear with all this. The Son is not only the Heir of all creation; He is the One who spoke it all into existence from Genesis 1:1*ff*.

Appendix F
The sons of God and Satan
Job 1:6

"Now there was a day when the **sons of God** came to present themselves before the LORD, and **Satan** also came among them. ⁷ And the LORD said to Satan, "From where do you come?" Then Satan answered the LORD and said, "From roaming about on the earth and walking around on it." ⁸ And the LORD said to Satan, "Have you considered My servant Job? For there is no one like him on the earth, a blameless and upright man, fearing God and turning away from evil" (Job 1:6-8).

The term sons of God used in Job are angelic beings or creatures.[1] However, there is a vast distinction between the 'sons of God' and Satan, the deceiver (Job 1:6; 2:1). The Hebrew word for Satan is שָׂטָן (transliterated *satan*) 1. adversary. 2. Satan[2] from the verbal root שָׂטַן ... be or act as adversary;[3] From the LXX ὁ διάβολος (Job 1:6 LXX); διάβολος, ον ... pertaining to engagement in slander, *slanderous* ...one who engages in slander ...title of the principal transcendent evil being *the adversary/devil,* already current in the LXX as translation of הַשָּׂטָן[4].

---

[1] It must be noted that the term 'sons of God' in Genesis refers to Godly men not angelic beings.
[2] Francis Brown, Samuel Rolles Driver, and Charles Augustus Briggs, <u>Enhanced Brown-Driver-Briggs Hebrew and English Lexicon</u> (Oxford: Clarendon Press, 1977), 966.
[3] Ibid.
[4] William Arndt, Frederick W. Danker, and Walter Bauer, <u>A Greek-English Lexicon of the New Testament and Other Early Christian Literature</u> (Chicago: University of Chicago Press, 2000), 226–227.

"Now there was a day when the **sons of God** came to present themselves before the LORD, and **Satan also came among them**" (Job 1:6).

וַיְהִי הַיּוֹם וַיָּבֹאוּ בְּנֵי הָאֱלֹהִים לְהִתְיַצֵּב עַל־יְהוָה וַיָּבוֹא גַם־הַשָּׂטָן בְּתוֹכָם:

1. Now there was a day when the sons of God came to present themselves before the LORD,
2. and the Satan גַם־הַשָּׂטָן (literally the deceiver with the article from Hebrew) also came וַיָּבוֹא among them בְּתוֹכָם
3. καὶ ὁ διάβολος ἦλθεν μετ' αὐτῶν (LXX) Note that the use of articulation in the Septuagint

Note the content of what is being established. The **sons of God** בְּנֵי הָאֱלֹהִים came to present themselves לְהִתְיַצֵּב (לְ particle preposition with יצב verb hithpael infinitive construct) from יָצַב verb only **hithpael... set** or station oneself, take one's stand ... עַל Job 1:6; 2:1[5] before the LORD. As the sons of God (angelic beings) were presenting themselves before God, the 'Satan, deceiver, accuser, etc.' came in among them. It may be translated with them but he is certainly isolated as being independent of them (*the construction of 1:6 will be compared to 2:1*). The belief that all 'the sons of God' were 'Satans, deceivers, accusers, etc.' evil angelic beings' just because 'the Satan' entered in their midst does grave violence to the Text.

Note also the verb יצב with the construct לְהִתְיַצֵּב (לְ particle preposition with יצב verb hithpael infinitive construct) is not used with 'the Satan.' He comes in 'among' them yet

---

[5] Francis Brown, Samuel Rolles Driver, and Charles Augustus Briggs, *Enhanced Brown-Driver-Briggs Hebrew and English Lexicon* (Oxford: Clarendon Press, 1977), 426.

very independent of them, and he is singled out in the Text especially with articulation. To believe all of 'them is with him' or 'him with them' by nature or character cannot be supported especially with this construction anywhere in the Text. The sons of God are definitely not 'the Satans' as many seem to believe.

"Sons of God "בְּנֵי הָאֱלֹהִים as the name of the celestial spirits, is also found outside of the book of Job (Gen. 6:2; cf. Ps. 29:1, 59:7, Dan. 3:25). They are so called, as beings in the likeness of God, which came forth from God in the earliest beginning of creation, before this material world and man came into existence (Job 28:4–7): the designation בְּנֵי points to the particular manner of their creation. (2.) Further, it is the teaching of Scripture, that these are the nearest attendants upon God, the nearest created glory, with which He has surrounded himself in His eternal glory, and that He uses them as the immediate instruments of His cosmical rule. This representation underlies Gen. 1:26, which Philo correctly explains, διαλέγεται ὁ τῶν ὅλων πατὴρ ταῖς ἑαυτοῦ δυνάμεσιν; and in Ps. 59:6–8, a psalm which is closely allied to the book of Job, קָהָל and סוֹד, of the holy ones, is just the assembly of the heavenly spirits, from which, as ἄγγελοι of God, they go forth into the universe and among men. (3.) It is also further the teaching of Scripture, that one of these spirits has withdrawn himself from the love of God, has reversed the truth of his bright existence, and in sullen ardent self-love is become the enemy of God, and everything godlike in the creature. This spirit is called, in reference to God and the creature, הַשָּׂטָן, from the verb שָׂטַן, to come in the way, oppose, treat with enmity,—a name which occurs first here, and except here occurs only in Zech. 3 and 1 Chron. 21:1. ... *Then Jehovah said to Satan, Whence comest thou? Satan answered Jehovah, and said, From going to and fro in the earth, and from walking up and down in it.* **Job 1:7.** … It is implied in the question that his business is selfish, arbitrary, and has no connection with God."[6]

It can be deduced from the immediate context that Satan has been arbitrarily scouting the earth doing things contrary to God's will. For the next few verses confirm that Satan is being challenged to possibly accuse (find fault with) a God fearing man in some manner. It must be continually noted that only the deceiver is being challenged not the others who are the sons of God (those destined to bring glory to their Creator). Just this one vile and evil angel who is no longer considered a son of God, he is singled out. He has become the slanderer, the devil, the accuser of the brethren.

"And the LORD said to Satan, "Have you considered My servant Job? For there is no one like him on the earth, a blameless and upright man, fearing God and turning away from evil." [9] Then Satan answered the LORD, "Does Job fear God for nothing?" (Job 1:8-9)

With these verses there is a challenge by God concerning Job who was a truly just and righteous man singled out and commended by God Himself. In fact, there was no one like Job on the earth that was so blameless fearing God. The overwhelming disdain of Satan can easily be discerned as he challenges God with the statement 'does Job fear You for no reason at all?' Satan is not only implying but questions the true fear of God in Job is a façade or superficial. He is accusing Job of being a fraud. He is also challenging the Lord's affirmation

---

[6] Carl Friedrich Keil and Franz Delitzsch, *Commentary on the Old Testament*, vol. 4 (Peabody, MA: Hendrickson, 1996), 272–274.

about Job's being blameless and fearing God turning from evil.[7]

Satan is devious and deceitful with every jot and tittle of his speech and actions as he castigates Job's true nature and motives. Satan slanders Job to Jehovah with these very hateful words "Hast Thou not made a hedge about him and his house and all that he has, on every side? Thou hast blessed the work of his hands, and his possessions have increased in the land. But put forth Thy hand now and touch[8] all that he has; he will surely curse Thee to Thy face" (Job 1:10-11). The deceiver was very precise with his challenge to the Lord. He made it perfectly clear that if what Job had was touched or destroyed he will curse your very being. All God did was challenge the roaming slanderer to consider Job with his deceptions and accusations. Satan is actually accusing the Lord of being deceived by Job and his supposed blameless life.

The sons of God were in no way being challenged with any of this. Only 'the Satan' is being addressed not the sons of God. They were just presenting themselves to the One they were serving and glorifying. Perhaps the Satan was there to try and corrupt some other celestial beings?

The sons of God and Satan

Job 2:1

"Again there was a day when the **sons of God** came to present themselves before the LORD, **and Satan also came**

---

[7] The fear of God can be defined biblically as 'to hate the evil and chose the good.' Many verses support this especially Proverbs 8:13 "The fear of the LORD is to hate evil; Pride and arrogance and the evil way, and the perverted mouth, I hate" (Prov. 8:13). Note also Isaiah 7:15 "He will eat curds and honey at the time He knows *enough* to refuse evil and choose good" (Is. 7:15).

[8] נָגַע ... touch, reach, strike ...of divine chastisement ... Jb 1:11; Francis Brown, Samuel Rolles Driver, and Charles Augustus Briggs, *Enhanced Brown-Driver-Briggs Hebrew and English Lexicon* (Oxford: Clarendon Press, 1977), 619.

among them to present himself before the LORD" (Job 2:1).

וַיְהִ֣י הַיּ֔וֹם וַיָּבֹ֙אוּ֙ בְּנֵ֣י הָאֱלֹהִ֔ים לְהִתְיַצֵּ֖ב עַל־יְהוָ֑ה וַיָּב֧וֹא גַֽם־הַשָּׂטָ֛ן בְּתֹכָ֖ם לְהִתְיַצֵּ֥ב עַל־יְהוָֽה׃

Job 2:1 is very similar to 1:6 but not exactly. There are several differences which add to prove that the sons of God are not associated with Satan.

1. Again there was a day when the **sons of God** came וַיָּבֹ֙אוּ֙ **to present themselves** before the LORD עַל־יְהוָ֑ה,
2. and **Satan** גַֽם־הַשָּׂטָ֛ן also came וַיָּב֧וֹא **among them** בְּתֹכָ֖ם **to present himself** לְהִתְיַצֵּ֥ב before the LORD עַל־יְהוָֽה" (Job 2:1).

It must be noted that Job 1:6 and 2:1 are identically posited in the Hebrew Text, "Now there was a day when the sons of God came to present themselves before the LORD" (Job 1:6; 2:1). The translation/s may vary but the Hebrew is absolutely identical. The second part of 2:1 presents more proof that the Satan was completely separate from the sons of God.

1. and **Satan** גַֽם־הַשָּׂטָ֛ן also came וַיָּב֧וֹא
2. **among them** בְּתֹכָ֖ם
3. **to present himself** לְהִתְיַצֵּ֥ב
4. before the LORD עַל־יְהוָֽה" (Job 2:1).

Note well that Satan presented himself independently of the sons of God presenting themselves. The verbs truly support this as the sons of God 'came' וַיָּבֹ֙אוּ֙ and Satan 'he came' וַיָּב֧וֹא and both are used with separate yet identical infinitive constructs לְהִתְיַצֵּ֥ב. The Text truly supports a separate 'presenting' before the Lord

What happens now further confirms the separation of the godly 'sons of God' and the godless 'the Satan.'

> "And the LORD said to Satan, "Where have you come from?" Then Satan answered the LORD and said, "From roaming about on the earth, and walking around on it." [3] And the LORD said to Satan, "Have you considered My servant Job? For there is no one like him on the earth, a blameless and upright man fearing God and turning away from evil. And he still holds fast his integrity, although you incited Me against him, to ruin him without cause." [4] And Satan answered the LORD and said, "Skin for skin! Yes, all that a man has he will give for his life. [5] "However, put forth Thy hand, now, and touch his bone and his flesh; he will curse Thee to Thy face" (Job 2:2-5).

This is almost identical to the first encounter with Satan concerning Job. (Job 1:1-12). God made it clear that even though Satan had brought all sorts of ruin against Job, Job had remained faithful to the Lord with great integrity. He did not curse God. Note well there is absolutely no charge against the other angels (sons of God) in any manner thus proving they were not in league with Satan or any of his evil schemes. They were and are never associated with any of the evil of Satan for they are true celestial sons of God. To even hint that the sons of God were conspirators with Satan certainly misses the truth of this Text.

Satan now makes another false accusation that if he were allowed to take away everything of Job, even Job's health almost unto death, Job would curse his Creator.

> So the LORD said to Satan, "Behold, he is in your power, only spare his life." [7] Then Satan went out from the presence of the LORD,

and smote Job with sore boils from the sole of his foot to the crown of his head" (Job 2:6-7).

"In Satan's second test he again indicted God's words and impugned Job's motives and character (cf. 1:6–8). The Hebrew for **without any reason is** *ḥinnām*, the same word **Satan** had used in 1:9. Though **Satan** accused **Job** of having an ulterior motive in his worship, **God** threw this back at the accuser, saying that Satan had *no* reason to incite God against the patriarch. In this third scene, back in heaven, **Satan** implied that Job was still worshiping God because he had not yet given up his life. **Skin for skin! A man will give all he has**—possessions and children—**for his own life**. "Skin for skin" was a proverbial saying, possibly about bartering or trading animal skins. Satan insinuated that Job had willingly traded the skins (lives) of his own children because in return God had given him his own skin (life). This again implied that Job was selfish. 2:5–6. **Satan** suggested that if Job were made to suffer physically, he would **curse** God to His **face** (cf. 1:11) for Job would have no reason for worship. He would see that God was against him. Surprisingly **the LORD** permitted Satan to afflict Job but not to kill him. God knew that Job would not deny Him."[9]

Conclusion

There was a time at the very beginning of creation when the Son of God created everything even the angelic host, the sons of God. "For by Him all things were created, *both* in the heavens and on earth, visible and invisible, whether thrones or dominions or rulers or authorities-- all things have been created by Him and for Him" (Col 1:16). And there was also a rejoicing among the entire heavenly host at creation.

"Where were you when I laid the foundation of the earth? Tell *Me*, if you have

---

[9] Roy B. Zuck, "Job," in *The Bible Knowledge Commentary: An Exposition of the Scriptures*, ed. J. F. Walvoord and R. B. Zuck, vol. 1 (Wheaton, IL: Victor Books, 1985), 721.

understanding, Who set its measurements, since you know? Or who stretched the line on it? On what were its bases sunk? Or who laid its cornerstone, when the morning stars sang together, **and all the sons of God shouted for joy**?" (Job 38:4-7).

It did not take very long that there was a rebellion in heaven and Satan a cherub took some of the angels with him. Satan has his angels who will be judged and for whom the eternal lake of fire was prepared, not for man. God has His angels who are the sons of God in Job.

"And the great dragon was thrown down, the serpent of old who is called **the devil and Satan**, who deceives the whole world; he was thrown down to the earth, **and his angels** were thrown down with him" (Rev 12:9).

"Then He will also say to those on His left, 'Depart from Me, accursed ones, into the eternal fire which has been prepared for **the devil and his angels**" (Mat. 25:41). τότε ἐρεῖ καὶ τοῖς ἐξ εὐωνύμων· πορεύεσθε ἀπ' ἐμοῦ [οἱ] κατηραμένοι εἰς τὸ πῦρ τὸ αἰώνιον τὸ ἡτοιμασμένον **τῷ διαβόλῳ καὶ τοῖς ἀγγέλοις αὐτοῦ.**

God's angels are elect or chosen angels who never sinned. **"The elect angels** (των ἐκλεκτων ἀγγελων [*tōn eklektōn aggelōn*])... "Elect" in the sense of the "holy" angels who kept their own principality (Jude 6) and who did not sin (2 Pet. 2:4)."[10]

---

[10] A.T. Robertson, *Word Pictures in the New Testament* (Nashville, TN: Broadman Press, 1933), 1 Ti 5:21.

"I solemnly charge you in the presence of God and of Christ Jesus and of *His* **chosen angels**, to maintain these *principles* without bias, doing nothing in a *spirit of* partiality" (1 Tim. 5:21). Διαμαρτύρομαι ἐνώπιον τοῦ θεοῦ καὶ Χριστοῦ Ἰησοῦ καὶ τῶν **ἐκλεκτῶν ἀγγέλων**, ἵνα ταῦτα φυλάξῃς χωρὶς προκρίματος, μηδὲν ποιῶν κατὰ πρόσκλισιν.

In the book of Job, the sons of God are the Lord's holy or elect angels who never sinned. They are wholly His and they have nothing in common with the evil one except they are all angels.

Made in the USA
Columbia, SC
16 November 2021